MY WELLBEING JOURNEY 2

Junior Cycle SPHE

Catherine Deegan
& Edel O'Brien

Gill Education
Hume Avenue
Park West
Dublin 12
www.gilleducation.ie

Gill Education is an imprint of M.H. Gill & Co.

© Catherine Deegan and Edel O'Brien 2019

ISBN: 978-0-7171-84286

Design: Síofra Murphy

Illustrations: Oxford Designers & Illustrators, Derry Dillon

At the time of going to press, all web addresses were active and contained information relevant to the topics in this book. Gill Education does not, however, accept responsibility for the content or views contained on these websites. Content, views and addresses may change beyond the publisher or author's control. Students should always be supervised when reviewing websites.

The authors and publisher are grateful to the following for permission to reproduce copyrighted material:

'Faced with the sober reality of a drunken night out with our teens' by Emma Blain. Copyright © Emma Blain, *The Sunday Independent*, 2007. Reproduced with permission of *The Sunday Independent*. Text adapted from *Resilience: Bouncing Back When Times Get Tough* by Anne Gillan, Lifelong Learning Teaching Tool bounceback.com.au

For permission to reproduce photographs, the authors and publisher gratefully acknowledge the following:

© Alamy: 14, 62C, 62R, 84L, 84CL, 84CR, 84R, 172T, 188TL, 188C, 190, 197BR; © Corbis: 40CB; © DigitalVision: 40T; © DigitalVision Vectors: 10, 64B, 74, 136B; © E+: 8L, 25TL, 26, 32B, 41, 64TR, 84C, 94B, 100, 106, 121TL, 143C; Image Source: 121C; Courtesy of Irish Water Safety (iws.ie): 46; © iStock: 1, 25CL, 25B, 25TR, 25C, 25CR, 27, 40CT, 40B, 47, 48, 49, 57, 58, 61, 63, 64TL, 73, 83, 93, 94T, 94C, 95, 99, 110, 112, 120, 121CR, 121TR, 132, 136C, 137, 143L, 151, 152, 160, 170, 172B, 173, 178, 182, 191, 197CR, 197BC, 198, 209, 210; © Moment: 82; Courtesy of Royal National Lifeboat Institution: 50; © Shutterstock: 8R, 62L, 62CL, 62CR ,130, 143R, 187, 188TR, 188CR, 197CL, 212; © Stockbyte: 121CL

The authors and publisher have made every effort to trace all copyright holders, but if any have been inadvertently overlooked we would be pleased to make the necessary arrangement at the first opportunity.

CONTENTS

INTRODUCTION
to My Wellbeing Journey 2

Welcome to *My Wellbeing Journey 2*! We hope you enjoyed following this programme over the last year and that it has helped you to learn more about and prioritise your health and wellbeing!

SPHE supports each of the six indicators of Wellbeing:

 active   responsible   connected   resilient   respected   aware

For that reason, SPHE and *My Wellbeing Journey* contributes significantly to your school's Wellbeing programme.

SPHE gives you the chance to develop a positive sense of self and the skills and insights for caring for yourself and others. You'll learn to make informed decisions about health and wellbeing and you will develop the resilience needed to cope with some of the challenges of the teenage years.

SPHE and *My Wellbeing Journey* put you at the centre of the learning experience. The active learning methods used throughout this series encourage you to engage fully with the topics discussed. We hope that the activities presented in *My Wellbeing Journey* will make for fun, thought-provoking and valuable SPHE classes.

Catherine Deegan and Edel O'Brien

Using *My Wellbeing Journey 2*

Specification links

My Wellbeing Journey is clearly linked to the SPHE specification. Not only is the book broken into four colour-coded strands but each lesson is linked to a specific Learning Outcome and Wellbeing Indicator. Learning Outcomes are then broken down further into student-friendly learning intentions.

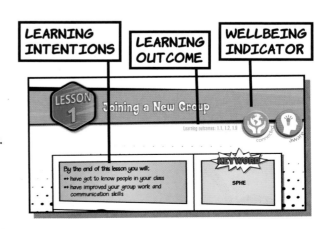

This very clear curriculum mapping will support planning. It will also assist the assessment process as you need to make sure that the Classroom-Based Assessment is based on Learning Outcomes from more than one strand.

Development of Key Skills

Each activity in the book supports the development of at least one of the Junior Cycle Key Skills. Icons indicate which Key Skill is addressed.

| Being Literate | Communicating | Being Creative | Managing Information & Thinking | Managing Myself | Being Numerate | Staying Well | Working with Others |

Meanwhile the words underneath the icon show what element or aspect of the Key Skill is being developed.

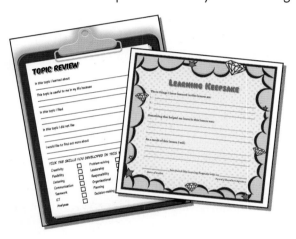

Reflection

Reflecting on learning is an important aspect of the Junior Cycle Framework. The Learning Keepsakes at the end of each lesson provide scaffolding for regular reflection. These reflections are particularly useful when it comes to deciding on a CBA in 2nd or 3rd year and for supporting communication with parents. Additional Topic Reviews are available on GillExplore and provide more opportunities for reflection.

Assessment

Meet the Challenges, linked to specific Learning Outcomes, Key Skills and Wellbeing Indicators and with clear success criteria, help prepare you for the Classroom-Based Assessment. They are particularly intended for people following the SPHE Short Course but provide engaging assessment opportunities for all SPHE students. A special Assessment section on page ix of this book will also guide you through the process of completing a successful CBA.

Additional resources

Numerous resources (including videos and PowerPoints) which support teaching and learning in SPHE are included on GillExplore.ie. The *My Wellbeing Journey Teacher's Resource Book* includes useful lesson planning material and schemes of work.

Following the SPHE course using *My Wellbeing Journey*

Your school has a choice in how it implements SPHE. You can:

- stick with the older modular SPHE curriculum (70 hours), first rolled out in 2000

- follow the newer SPHE short course (100 hours), developed under the new Junior Cycle Framework in 2016

- develop your own, purpose-built SPHE short course that meets requirements (e.g. is at least 70 hours long)

All of the choices can seem quite confusing but the *My Wellbeing Journey* series is flexible so that it can be used whatever option you take. The series fully covers both the NCCA-developed modular and short courses. All activities in *My Wellbeing Journey* specifically nurture different Key Skill elements, while all lessons are mapped to relevant Statements of Learning and Wellbeing Indicators, to help ensure you are in line with the Junior Cycle Framework.

How *My Wellbeing Journey 2* helps you fulfil the Learning Outcomes of the SPHE Short Course

The table below highlights where the various Learning Outcomes are addressed in this book. This list of Learning Outcomes is also important as you will need to make sure that your CBA addresses Learning Outcomes from at least two different strands.

STRAND 1: WHO AM I?

STUDENTS SHOULD BE ABLE TO	RELEVANT LESSONS
1.1 appreciate the importance of building their own self-esteem and that of others	See *My Wellbeing Journey 1* and *3*
1.2 welcome individual difference based on an appreciation of their own uniqueness	See *My Wellbeing Journey 1*
1.3 participate in informed discussions about the impact of physical, emotional, psychological and social development in adolescence	Lesson 4
1.4 recognise how sexuality and gender identity is part of what it means to be human and has biological, psychological, cultural, social and spiritual dimensions	Lesson 28
1.5 identify short, medium and long-term personal goals and ways in which they might be achieved	Lessons 2, 3, 5
1.6 apply decision-making skills in a variety of situations	Lessons 6, 8
1.7 source appropriate and reliable information about health and wellbeing	Lessons 7, 8, 9, 10
1.8 explain how stereotyping can contribute to a person's understanding and experience of rights and wellbeing	Lesson 12
1.9 appreciate the importance of respectful and inclusive behaviour in promoting a safe environment free from bias and discrimination	Lessons 1, 11, 12

STRAND 2: MINDING MYSELF AND OTHERS

STUDENTS SHOULD BE ABLE TO	RELEVANT LESSONS
2.1 evaluate how diet, physical activity, sleep/rest and hygiene contribute to self-confidence, self-esteem and wellbeing	Lessons 13, 14, 15
2.2 critique the impact of the media, advertising and other influences on one's decisions about health and wellbeing	Lesson 30; see *My Wellbeing Journey 3*
2.3 describe what promotes a sense of belonging in school, at home and in the wider community and their own role in creating an inclusive environment	Lesson 16
2.4 distinguish between appropriate care giving and receiving	See *My Wellbeing Journey 3*
2.5 demonstrate the personal and social skills to address pressure to smoke, to drink alcohol and/or use other substances	Lessons 6, 19, 21, 22, 24
2.6 reflect on the personal, social and legal consequences of their own or others' drug use	Lessons 20, 21, 22
2.7 critique information and supports available for young people in relation to substance use	See *My Wellbeing Journey 3*
2.8 use the skills of active listening and responding appropriately in a variety of contexts	Lesson 19
2.9 use good communication skills to respond to criticism and conflict	Lesson 19
2.10 describe appropriate responses to incidents of bullying	Lesson 18
2.11 appraise the roles of participants and bystanders in incidents of bullying	Lesson 18
2.12 review the school's anti-bullying policy and internet safety guidelines explaining the implications for students' behaviour and personal safety	Lesson 17

STRAND 3: TEAM UP

STUDENTS SHOULD BE ABLE TO	RELEVANT LESSONS
3.1 establish what young people value in different relationships and how this changes over time	Lesson 23
3.2 evaluate attitudes, skills and values that help to make, maintain and end friendships respectfully	Lesson 23
3.3 recognise their capacity to extend and receive friendship	See *My Wellbeing Journey 1* and *3*
3.4 explain the different influences on relationships and levels of intimacy	Lessons 24, 25
3.5 analyse relationship difficulties experienced by young people	Lesson 26
3.6 describe fertility, conception, pre-natal development and birth, and the particular health considerations for each	Lesson 27
3.7 explain what it means to take care of their sexual health	See *My Wellbeing Journey 3*
3.8 demonstrate assertive communication skills in support of responsible, informed decision-making about relationships and sexual health that are age and developmentally appropriate	See *My Wellbeing Journey 3*
3.9 reflect on the personal and social dimensions of sexual orientation and gender identity	Lesson 28
3.10 critically analyse the use of sexual imagery and gender stereotyping in various forms of media	Lesson 31; see *My Wellbeing Journey 1* and *3*
3.11 critique the influence of media on their understanding of sexuality and sexual health	See *My Wellbeing Journey 3*

STRAND 4: MY MENTAL HEALTH

STUDENTS SHOULD BE ABLE TO	RELEVANT LESSONS
4.1 explain what it means to have positive mental health	See *My Wellbeing Journey 1*
4.2 appreciate the importance of talking things over, including recognising the links between thoughts, feelings and behaviour	Lessons 29, 30, 31
4.3 practise some relaxation techniques	See *My Wellbeing Journey 1* and *3*
4.4 participate in an informed discussion about mental health issues experienced by young people and/or their friends and family	Lesson 32
4.5 appreciate what it means to live with mental ill-health	Lesson 32
4.6 critique mental health services available to young people locally	Lesson 32
4.7 explain the significance of substance use for one's mental health	Lesson 22
4.8 practise a range of strategies for building resilience	Lesson 33
4.9 use coping skills for managing life's challenges	Lesson 33
4.10 explain the wide range of life events where they might experience loss and bereavement	See *My Wellbeing Journey 1*
4.11 outline the personal, social, emotional and physical responses to loss and bereavement	Lesson 34
4.12 compare how loss and bereavement are portrayed in a variety of contexts and cultures	Lesson 34
4.13 describe how they might care for themselves and be supportive of others in times of loss or bereavement	Lesson 34

How *My Wellbeing Journey 2* helps you fulfil the SPHE Modular Curriculum

The older SPHE modular curriculum is prepared in ten modules, each of which appears in each year of the three-year cycle. Your school can still follow the modular course, if it prefers. However, if you are following the modular curriculum, you'll need to make sure that you are integrating key aspects of the Junior Cycle Framework, such as Statements of Learning, Key Skills and Wellbeing Indicators. As *My Wellbeing Journey* is written to be fully in line with the Junior Cycle Framework, all of this integration has been done for you.

MODULE	RELEVANT LESSONS
Belonging and Integrating	Lessons 1, 2, 11
Self-Management: A Sense of Purpose	Lessons 3, 5
Communication Skills	Lesson 19
Physical Health	Lessons 7, 13, 14, 15
Friendship	Lessons 17, 18, 23
Relationships and Sexuality	Lessons 4, 24, 25, 26, 27
Emotional Health	Lessons 29, 31
Influences and Decisions	Lessons 6, 30
Substance Use	Lessons 20, 21, 22
Personal Safety	Lessons 8, 9

Additional lessons: 10, 12, 16, 28, 32, 33, 34. These lessons have been written to fulfil the requirements of the new SPHE Short Course. If you are following the modular curriculum you mightn't have time to cover these new lessons and the additional assessment options (Meet the Challenges) provided in the book. Feel free to cover these lessons, if your context allows.

Assessment

If you are following the SPHE Short Course, your learning will be assessed in the form of one **Classroom-Based Assessment (CBA)**. This CBA can take place in either **Second or Third Year**, once you have completed learning in at least three strands. The outcome of your SPHE CBA will be reported on your **Junior Cycle Profile of Achievement**.

Classroom-Based Assessment: Advice for students

✔ **Choose a project that you are interested in learning more about**. If you are doing a group project, try to ensure that each member of the group is interested and cares about the topic being addressed.

✔ **Keep a record of the topics that interest you** as you go through the different strands of the SPHE short course. You can do this by completing your Learning Keepsakes. Look out for images, videos and written materials that will help you to learn more about this topic(s). These will also help you to make your project more interesting.

✔ **Your project will focus on learning in at least two strands of the SPHE short course**. Your book is broken into four strands, each differentiated by colour. It is a good idea to begin by making links between topics in the different strands. This will help you to choose a worthwhile project.

✔ When your teacher is helping you and your classmates to decide on a project for your CBA, **use information you have already gathered and do some further research to help you** encourage your group/class to consider doing the project that you think is **worthwhile**.

✔ Once the focus of the project has been decided, **identify sources of reliable information with your teacher**.

✔ **Divide the project tasks out** between the group in such a way that everybody can work to their strengths.

✔ **Use your creativity in both capturing and presenting your project**. You can complete your project as a document, a presentation, a video and/or through images.

✔ Your teacher will support you in planning and completing your project for the SPHE CBA.

✔ The **Features of Quality** will be used to provide you with feedback about **what you are doing well and what you can do to improve**.

✔ **Keep notes on what you are learning** as you complete the CBA by filling out the **Planning and Preparation template** on the following pages. These notes will help you complete a quality reflection about your learning in the project.

Sample Projects for Classroom-Based Assessments
(adapted from www.curriculumonline.ie)

Here are some examples that might help you to come up with a project for your SPHE CBA. You might also look to the **Meet the Challenges** in your books for some inspiration!

PROJECT	STRANDS AND LEARNING OUTCOMES	SUCCESS CRITERIA
Sample 1 Design a resource for your peers called 'Aid to Decision-Making'.	**Strand 1:** 1.5, 1.6, 1.7 **Strand 2:** 2.1, 2.6, 2.7	1. Decide on the type of resource you will make. 2. Identify what materials and resources you will need for your resource. 3. Include a decision-making model or steps for making a good decision in your resource. 4. Highlight the important areas where good decision-making is important for young people, e.g. diet, substance use, studying, etc. 5. Include the names of organisations, websites and/or helplines that have information on the topics you are focussing on. 6. Decide on a format for your resource, e.g. will you make a booklet, write a blog or create a short film? 7. Use language, images, etc. that are suitable for and will appeal to young people. 8. Complete your Reflection Sheet. *(See section 'E. Showing evidence of meaningful reflection', p. xv.)*
Sample 2 Contribute to an advertising campaign on 'Adolescence: The age of opportunity'	**Strand 1:** 1.2, 1.4, 1.5, 1.9 **Strand 2:** 2.3, 2.5, 2.7, 2.8, 2.9, 2.10 **Strand 3:** 3.2, 3.3, 3.8, 3.9 **Strand 4:** 4.1, 4.2, 4.8, 4.9	1. Decide on the main purpose and message of your advertising campaign. 2. Decide on your audience and how best to get the message out to them. 3. Consider whether you might create a print/online/radio or TV campaign. 4. Outline some of the changes that occur in adolescence, e.g. new school, meeting new people, more responsibility, more freedom, new experiences, etc. 5. Give the advantages and challenges involved in some of these changes, e.g. being accepted, making new friends, assessments and tests, following your interests, peer pressure, etc. 6. Outline the skills adolescences can develop to meet the challenges they face, e.g. good communication skills, building their self-esteem, etc. 7. Provide the names of helplines and information sites for young people.
Sample 3 Design a media campaign about the consequences of alcohol and tobacco use and where and how to get help for drug-related problems	**Strand 2:** 2.5, 2.6, 2.7 **Strand 4:** 4.7, 4.8, 4.9	1. Decide who your target audience is. 2. Develop the key messages of your campaign. 3. Consider how you will best get your message across. Your campaign might include interviews, articles, short documentaries, viral social media clips, publicising important research or getting endorsements from well-known people. 4. Research relevant helping organisations. 5. Outline the different pressures that young people feel around substance abuse. 6. Highlight consequences of substance misuse, e.g. personal, social and legal.

Features of Quality

Your CBA will be assessed according to the following **Features of Quality**. Your teacher(s) will assign a descriptor to your CBA depending on what description best fits your CBA. It is a good idea to familiarise yourself with the Features of Quality.

DESCRIPTOR	FEATURES OF QUALITY FOR SPHE PROJECT AND REFLECTION
Exceptional	• The project reflects excellent use of background information. • It demonstrates an excellent level of creativity and original interpretation of the material. • It shows excellent awareness of audience, where this is relevant to the project. • There is substantial evidence of meaningful reflection on their learning.
Above expectations	• The project reflects very clear use of background information. • It demonstrates a very high level of creativity and original interpretation of the material. • It shows a clear awareness of audience, where this is relevant to the project. • There is strong evidence of meaningful reflection on their learning.
In line with expectations	• The project reflects satisfactory use of background information. • It demonstrates a satisfactory level of creativity in the design of the project. • It shows satisfactory awareness of audience, where this is relevant to the project. • There is good evidence of reflection on their learning.
Yet to meet expectations	• The project reflects a limited understanding of the background information. • Creativity or an ability to interpret the material in the design of the project is missing. • It lacks an awareness of audience where this is relevant to the project. • There is little evidence of reflection on their learning.

Classroom-Based Assessment Planning and Preparation template

Fill in the following template as you plan and carry out your CBA. Doing this will help ensure you address all Features of Quality and produce an interesting and meaningful CBA.

A. Deciding on a project

First, list the topics that you found most interesting in your SPHE class:

_____

_____

Look back at the four strands covered in SPHE (have a look at the contents pages if you're unsure of what topics fall under which strands). Then tick which strands you would like to cover as part of your CBA:

- ☐ Strand 1: Who Am I?
- ☐ Strand 2: Minding Myself and Others
- ☐ Strand 3: Team Up
- ☐ Strand 4: My Mental Health

Now list the specific learning outcomes you would like to address in your CBA. Make sure you include at least one learning outcome from two different strands. You'll find the relevant learning outcomes listed at the start of each lesson and also in a table at the front of this book.

_____

What would you like to achieve through your CBA?

_____

How will you present your information/project? Tick the relevant box or describe below.

- ☐ Advertising campaign
- ☐ Media campaign
- ☐ Display board
- ☐ Presentation
- ☐ Event
- ☐ Poster/Infographic
- ☐ Video
- ☐ Podcast
- ☐ Publication (booklet, book, magazine, newsletter)
- ☐ Other: _____

How will you divide up the work involved in the project?

_____

_____

Describe your particular role in the project:

_____

_____

_____

B. Gathering background information

You need to source and use good quality background information on the topic of your CBA. To do this you should:

- ☐ Research and use at least three different sources of information
- ☐ Make sure your information comes from good quality sources. (Ask yourself if the information comes from a reliable source or if it might be biased in some way. Also consider how old the source of information is and if it is relevant to your particular project.)
- ☐ Try to check that your information is correct by verifying it against different sources
- ☐ Use different types of sources

Look at the following types of sources and circle the types you will try to use:

| Newspapers/magazines | Books | Websites | Information leaflets |

| Videos | Photographs | Audio recordings | Libraries | Interviews |

| Surveys | Visits to local information centres | Data sources (e.g. relevant statistics) |

Others: _____

Now pick out your top three sources and describe the useful information you found in each source.

Source 1: _____

Useful information from Source 1:

_____

_____

_____

How do you know this information is reliable?

_____

_____

Source 2: _____

Useful information from Source 2:

_____

_____

_____

How do you know this information is reliable?

_____

_____

Source 3: _____

Useful information from Source 3:

_____

_____

_____

How do you know this information is reliable?

_____

_____

C. Showing creativity and original interpretation

Presentation

Think about other projects and resources you have seen on this topic. How will your presentation of information be different and unique?

- ☐ I will use a **form of presentation** that has never been used before for this topic.
- ☐ I will present the information in a way that is **much more suitable for my target audience.**
- ☐ I will present the information from a **unique viewpoint.**
- ☐ I will use **artistic skills** to present the project in a unique way.
- ☐ Other: _____

Explain how the **presentation** of your project will be unique and show excellent levels of creativity:

_____

_____

Original interpretation of material

What will be original about the content of your project?

- ☐ I will look at the topic from a **local perspective.**
- ☐ I will include **original data** (I will carry out my own surveys, interviews, etc.)
- ☐ I will engage with the topic and provide my **own opinions.**
- ☐ Other: _____

Explain how you will interpret information in an original way:

_____

_____

As you complete your CBA, explain what makes your project on this topic different from other projects on similar topics:

_____

_____

D. Showing awareness of audience

Describe your target audience.

_____

List three things you will do to make your project relevant and interesting to your target audience.

1. _____

2. _____

3. _____

E. Showing evidence of meaningful reflection

When you have finished your project you must complete a reflection on the work you carried out. Your reflection will be taken into account when your project is being assessed.

You must complete an individual reflection, even if you worked with a group on your CBA. Reflections may be completed in oral or written form.

Use the Sample Reflection Sheet on the next page or the following sentences to help you complete your reflection:

In this project, I was/we were asked to …

In completing this project, the best sources of information were … because …

My particular contribution to the project was …

By doing this project I learned the following about this topic …

Completing this project has influenced my thinking/behaviour/attitudes in the following ways: …

I think that this learning is important for young people because …

Sample Reflection Sheet

Strands:_____

Topic: _____

Outline of the project:_____

_____

How I/we completed the project:_____

_____

_____

Important information sourced and how I/we made decisions about what to include:

_____

_____

_____

My role in the project and what I did well: _____

_____

_____

What my group did well:_____

_____

_____

What I might do differently next time: _____

_____

_____

Challenges/obstacles encountered:_____

_____

_____

This project is important for young people because..._____

_____

_____

How would I apply what I have learned in my own life?_____

_____

_____

_____

WHO AM I?

STRAND 1

TOPIC 1
How I See Myself and Others

LESSON 1 — Class Contract

Learning outcome: 1.9

responsible   connected   respected   aware

By the end of this lesson you will:

→ have drawn up a set of ground rules to help your SPHE class work well together

KEYWORDS

Ground rules
Class contract

Developing good
relationships

GROUP ACTIVITY

This is Ms Doyle's SPHE class. She
has written some words on the board
about what helps the class to run
well. As a class, discuss how each
word would help an SPHE class work
efficiently. Then, in groups, think of
a ground rule to go with each word.
The first one has been done for you.

Respect

Confidentiality

Responsibility

Freedom

Participation

Organisation

Punctuality

WORDS	GROUND RULES
RESPECT	I will listen to others when they are speaking.
CONFIDENTIALITY	
RESPONSIBILITY	
FREEDOM	
PARTICIPATION	
ORGANISATION	
PUNCTUALITY	

CLASS ACTIVITY

Respecting difference; Learning with others

Choose a reporter from your group to share your group's ground rules with the rest of the class. The whole class must now agree on a set of ground rules. Ensure that each ground rule begins with an 'I' statement, e.g. 'I will listen to others when they are speaking.' When agreement has been reached on these ground rules, write them into the contract. Everyone must sign their own contract to show that they agree.

CLASS CONTRACT

CONTRACT

Signed: _____

LEARNING KEEPSAKE

Three things I have learned in this lesson are:

1. _____

2. _____

3. _____

Something that helped me learn in this lesson was:

_____

_____

_____

As a result of this lesson, I will:

_____

_____

_____

_____ has shared this Learning Keepsake with me _____

Name of student   *Parent's/Guardian's signature*

 **LESSON 2**

Looking Back, Looking Forward

Learning outcome: 1.5

 responsible

 resilient

 aware

By the end of this lesson you will:
- have reviewed First Year
- have identified your goals for Second Year

KEYWORDS

Challenge
Review

Looking back, looking forward

Looking back on First Year helps you to reflect on your achievements. It also helps you to make improvements in Second Year. Perhaps you would like to improve your grades, or maybe you would like to get involved in more extracurricular activities. The start of Second Year is a great opportunity for you to set goals and make decisions about what you want to achieve in the year ahead. Review your First Year in secondary school by filling in the sheet on the next page.

FIRST YEAR REVIEW SHEET

My two biggest highlights from first year were:

My biggest challenge was:

_____

_____

_____

_____

My biggest achievement in First Year was:

Four people who supported me were:

This year I am looking forward to:

_____

_____

_____

Looking forward to Third Year

At the end of Third Year, you will be awarded a Junior Cycle Profile of Achievement. This will show all the results you achieved in your Classroom-Based Assessments and the results/descriptors that you will have achieved in your academic subjects, e.g. English, Irish, Maths, etc. The descriptors for Junior Cycle are as follows:

Distinction	90%–100%
Higher Merit	75%–89%
Merit	55%–74%
Achieved	40%–54%
Partially achieved	20%–39%
Not graded	0%–19%

The Other Areas of Learning (OAL) section on your Profile of Achievement allows you to record the skills you have developed throughout the Junior Cycle. The skills you might develop through your participation in OAL include creativity, communication, leadership, teamwork, ICT and problem-solving. The most important thing to remember is that the OAL is school-based. Examples of suitable achievements for inclusion as an OAL are:

1. **Specific awards you have won for sporting or cultural achievements in First, Second or Third Year**
2. **Taking part in a charity fundraising event**
3. **Organising an awareness campaign in your school**
4. **Being part of any school club**
5. **Holding a leadership role, e.g. class representative or prefect**

Here are two sample entries for the OAL section of your Junior Cycle Profile of Achievement.

SAMPLE 1

Niema is a member of the school basketball team. This year, she reached the All-Ireland Final. This experience developed her communication skills as she had to listen to and follow her coach's instructions as well as communicate with her teammates. This experience also allowed her to achieve her personal targets and developed her self-confidence.

SAMPLE 2

Kris is a member of the Student Council. He organised a charity fundraiser for the homeless. This helped him to develop his problem-solving skills as he often had to reorganise meetings to take account of changes to other people's schedules. It also helped him to be creative and innovative as he had to come up with ideas for posters and for new ways to help raise money.

INDIVIDUAL ACTIVITY

Making considered decisions

In the Junior Cycle Profile of Achievement template below, fill in the subjects you do. Then write in the results you would like to achieve in your Junior Cycle. Complete the Other Areas of Learning section with what you would like to see written in your final assessment.

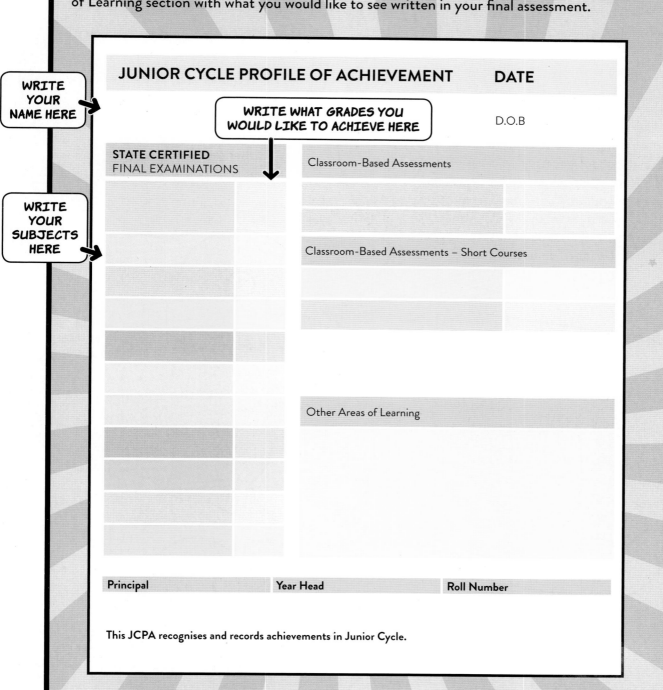

WRITE YOUR NAME HERE ➤

WRITE WHAT GRADES YOU WOULD LIKE TO ACHIEVE HERE ↓

WRITE YOUR SUBJECTS HERE ➤

JUNIOR CYCLE PROFILE OF ACHIEVEMENT

DATE

D.O.B

STATE CERTIFIED
FINAL EXAMINATIONS

Classroom-Based Assessments

Classroom-Based Assessments – Short Courses

Other Areas of Learning

Principal

Year Head

Roll Number

This JCPA recognises and records achievements in Junior Cycle.

Achieving my goals

Now that you have thought about what you want to achieve this year, it is important to set goals. Making a plan will help you meet your targets. Following the 'What, Why, When, How and Who' steps can help you to achieve your goals.

(1)

WHAT do you want to achieve?

Write down exactly what you want to achieve. Writing down your goal will help you to commit to it. It is important that your goal is specific and realistic – an unrealistic goal is impossible to achieve. When you are specific about your goal, it is easier to create a plan towards achieving it. An example of a specific goal is: 'I want to go from "Achieved" to "Merit" in maths by Christmas.' An example of a vague or unspecific goal is: 'I want to do better at maths.'

(2)

WHY do you want to achieve it?

Think about why you want to achieve this goal. Write down the reasons. The key to being successful is wanting to achieve the goal for yourself, and not just to please other people such as parents, teachers or coaches.

(3)

WHEN do you want to achieve it?

Give yourself a realistic timeframe within which to achieve your goal. Identify how much time you will need, then pick a start date.

(4)

HOW will you achieve it?

Think about the steps you need to take to achieve your goal. Write them down. Break a big goal into small, manageable steps. Tick off each step as you achieve it; this will give you the confidence and motivation to keep going. Write down anything that might stop you from achieving your goal.

(5)

WHO will help you achieve it?

Having supportive people around you is important. Think about the people in your life who will help you to achieve your goal.

INDIVIDUAL ACTIVITY

Setting and achieving
personal goals

Choose one of the goals you have set for your Junior Cycle Profile of Achievement. This can be from the subject section, the CBA section or the OAL section. On the roadmap below, fill in the necessary steps you must take to achieve this goal.

1. WHAT: THE GOAL I WANT TO ACHIEVE IS:

_____
_____
_____

2. WHY: TWO REASONS I WANT TO ACHIEVE THIS ARE:

_____
_____

3. WHEN: I WANT TO ACHIEVE MY GOAL BY:

_____
_____

4. HOW: THE STEPS I WILL TAKE TO ACHIEVE MY GOAL ARE:

_____
_____

THE THINGS THAT MIGHT STOP ME ACHIEVING MY GOAL ARE:

_____
_____

5. WHO: THE PEOPLE WHO WILL HELP ME TO ACHIEVE MY GOAL ARE:

_____
_____
_____

LEARNING KEEPSAKE

Three things I have learned in this lesson are:

1. _____

2. _____

3. _____

Something that helped me learn in this lesson was:

_____

_____

_____

As a result of this lesson, I will:

_____

_____

_____

_____ has shared this Learning Keepsake with me _____

Name of student   *Parent's/Guardian's signature*

LESSON 3

What Motivates Me?

Learning outcome: 1.5

responsible   resilient   respected   aware

By the end of this lesson you will:

→ have identified some of the people and supports in your life

→ understand the different aspects of motivation

KEYWORDS

Motivation
Encouragement

 INDIVIDUAL ACTIVITY

Reading for enjoyment and
with understanding

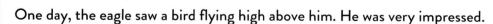

1. Read the following story and answer the questions that follow.

The Chicken and the Eagle

The story is told of a man who found an eagle's egg. He put it with his chicks and mother hens.

Soon the egg hatched. The young eagle grew up with all the other chickens. Whatever the chickens did, the eagle did too. He thought he was a chicken, just like them.

Since the chickens could only fly for a short distance, the eagle also learned to fly a short distance. He thought that was what he was supposed to do, so that was all that he thought he could do. And that was all he was able to do.

One day, the eagle saw a bird flying high above him. He was very impressed.

'Who is that?' he asked the hens around him.

'That's the eagle, the king of the birds,' the hens told him. 'He belongs to the sky. We belong to the earth – we are chickens.'

So the eagle lived and died a chicken, for that's what he thought he was.

13

(a) Who did the eagle admire in this story?

_____

_____

(b) Why was the eagle not motivated to fly like an eagle?

_____

_____

(c) What is the message of the story?

_____

_____

2. 'You may never fly like an eagle, but you will have your own hopes and dreams.' If you could achieve anything in life, what would it be and who could support you in achieving it?

_____

_____

What motivates me?

A. Motivators

Motivation is the reason or reasons for acting or behaving in a certain way. It can come from your own likes, desires and personal values (intrinsic motivation), e.g. if you value physical fitness, you might be motivated to go to the gym or to get involved in sports, or if you want good results in your exams, you might be motivated to put in extra study. Motivation can also come from others (extrinsic motivation), e.g. role models or events, such as your county winning the All-Ireland (you might be encouraged to train harder in the hopes of making the team one day).

Knowing myself

INDIVIDUAL ACTIVITY

On the stairs, write in who and what are the main motivators in your life. You may choose from the 'Motivators' list below or create your own. List your motivators in order of importance, with 1 being the most important motivator for you and 5 being the least important.

MOTIVATORS

Praise: Appreciation for achievements
Interest: The love of a subject, sport or hobby
Control: The ability to influence what happens
People: e.g. Role models and team members
Prizes: Winning

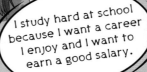

If I get good results in my history exam, my mother said I can go to the disco.

I study hard at school because I want a career I enjoy and I want to earn a good salary.

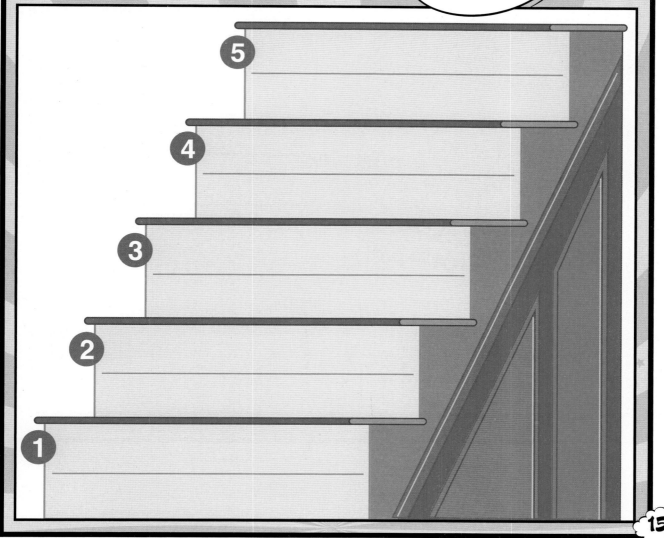

B. Goal-setting

Setting goals can help us to become motivated. A wish written down with a date becomes a goal. A goal broken down into steps becomes a plan. A plan backed by action becomes success.

INDIVIDUAL ACTIVITY

Setting goals

In the diagram below, fill in: a goal you would like to achieve; the reason why you want to achieve it (your motivation); when you want to achieve it by; what action you must take to achieve it.

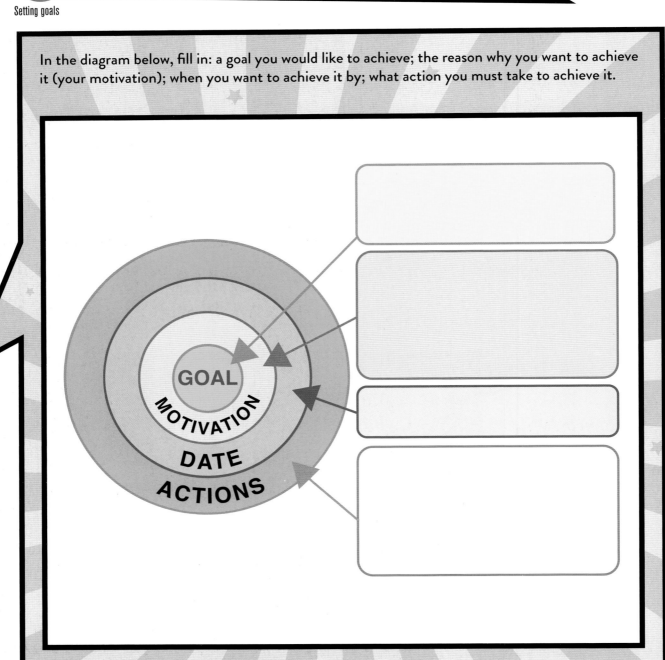

INDIVIDUAL ACTIVITY

Listening and
expressing myself

Answer the following questions:

1. What is the biggest motivating factor in your life?

2. Why does this motivate you?

3. How does this affect your work in school?

4. How does this affect your life outside school?

5. How might this affect the job you choose after school?

INDIVIDUAL ACTIVITY

Knowing myself

Research a job you are interested in and answer the following questions:

1. What are the main tasks of this job?

_____

_____

2. What would motivate you to do these tasks if you were doing this job?

_____

_____

3. Based on the things that motivates you, would this job suit you? Why?

_____

_____

LEARNING KEEPSAKE

Three things I have learned in this lesson are:

1. _____

2. _____

3. _____

Something that helped me learn in this lesson was:

_____

_____

_____

As a result of this lesson, I will:

_____

_____

_____

_____ has shared this Learning Keepsake with me _____

Name of student   *Parent's/Guardian's signature*

MEET THE CHALLENGE
Strand 1 Topic 1
INFORMATION LEAFLET FOR INCOMING FIRST YEARS

Learning outcomes: 2.3, 3.2, 3.3, 4.9

Create an information leaflet for incoming First Years to your school. The leaflet is designed to give the new First Years tips and advice on how to overcome the challenge of starting secondary school. Your leaflet should include information on:

- ○ the school
- ○ differences between primary and secondary school
- ○ what you found difficult about starting secondary school
- ○ how you overcame these difficulties
- ○ how to make new friends
- ○ how to feel part of the school community
- ○ how to manage your locker
- ○ supports available in the school
- ○ a map of the school building
- ○ any other information that you feel is important

TOPIC 2
Being an Adolescent

Being an Adolescent

active   responsible   connected   resilient   respected   aware

Learning outcome: 1.3

By the end of this lesson you will:

➡ have revised the different changes that occur in adolescence

➡ have discussed and debated the effects of these changes

KEYWORDS

Difference
Stereotype

Adolescence is the period following the onset of puberty, generally between the ages of 13 and 19. It is a time of great change. Physical changes occur due to the hormonal changes that take place during puberty. Social changes also occur as you begin to spend more time with your peers, while at home your parents may give you extra responsibilities and begin to expect more from you. Adolescence is an exciting time. For many young people, it brings increased freedom and new experiences. However, for some young people, adolescence can also be a very challenging time.

INDIVIDUAL ACTIVITY

Evaluating information and data

In First-Year SPHE, you studied and discussed many of the physical, emotional, psychological and social changes that occur in adolescence. Complete the crossword below to identify some of these changes.

Across

1. There is an increased growth of this on the body during puberty.
4. A skin condition which sometimes develops during puberty.
6. Relationships with these people change and become more important during adolescence.
9. Excessive sweating during puberty may cause this.
11. These feelings can develop towards others during adolescence.
12. A young person's fashion trends and behaviour can be influenced and shaped by this.

Down

2. The period following the onset of puberty during which a person develops from a child into an adult.
3. In order to be accepted by friends and class, a person may give in to this.
5. The desire to want to grow up and be free of parental restraints.
7. The perception a person has about themselves when they look in the mirror.
8. Frequent changes in a person's emotions.
10. A time of hormonal and physical change for teenagers.

CLASS DISCUSSION

Discussing/Debating

 # INDIVIDUAL ACTIVITY

Reading for enjoyment and
with understanding; Writing
for different purposes

1. Read this letter, written to the editor of a national newspaper, complaining about the youth of today.

OPINION

Dear Editor,

I feel the need to share a recent experience I had with teenagers. This experience was both frustrating and irritating, and it made wonder, what hope do we have if these teenagers are our future adults?

My experience began while waiting for my bus into the city centre. Sitting beside me at the bus stop were two teenagers who barely spoke to each other because they were totally engrossed in their phones. When the bus arrived, I was pushed out of the way by a moody teenager who was shouting down the phone, I presume to one of his poor parents, 'I'll be home when I'm ready!'

As I stepped onto the bus I began to cough: I was totally overwhelmed by the scent of deodorants and who knows what else. The whole bus seemed to be crowded with loud groups of teenagers, all of whom looked the same with their silly haircuts and clothes.

As the bus travelled into the city centre, a teenager started vaping. She passed it around to her friends so they were all puffing away on this one vape. I heard one kid say, 'No thanks', and then the whole group started making fun of him, so he wasn't long taking it off them and puffing away himself.

By the time I got off the bus, I was weary and disillusioned with the youth of today. Is this the behaviour of all teenagers or just the ones I had the misfortune of meeting today?

Yours etc.,

John Smith

2. Write a reply to this man's letter explaining what may have caused the teenagers to behave in the way they did. In your reply, include some of the challenges experienced during adolescence.

LEARNING KEEPSAKE

Three things I have learned in this lesson are:

1. _____

2. _____

3. _____

Something that helped me learn in this lesson was:

_____

_____

_____

As a result of this lesson, I will:

_____

_____

_____

_____ has shared this Learning Keepsake with me _____

Name of student   *Parent's/Guardian's signature*

MEET THE CHALLENGE
Strand 1 Topic 2
'BEING A TEENAGER' COMIC STRIP

Learning outcomes: 1.3, 1.4, 3.1, 3.2, 3.3, 3.4, 3.5, 4.1, 4.8

In pairs, create an eight-panel comic strip that highlights the changes and/or challenges and/or rewards of being a teenager.

○ Decide on what aspect of being a teenager you will focus on, e. g. a teenager who worries they are not growing up quickly enough, or a young person who was confident in primary school but who feels very self-conscious now that they are a teenager, or a teenager who is enjoying their increased freedom, etc.

○ Plan your story. Show how the teenager deals with their challenge/how the teenager is enjoying being an adolescent.

○ Now draw your panels.

○ Add an outline of your characters and include speech bubbles.

○ Add background details, e.g. trees, classroom clock, canteen, etc.

○ Write the dialogue. Try to have a balance between dialogue and images.

TOPIC 3
Self-Management

Study Skills

Learning outcome: 1.5

responsible

resilient

aware

By the end of this lesson you will:

➥ have practised effective study skills

KEYWORDS

Mind map
Flash cards
Mnemonics

USEFUL WEBSITES

www.how-to-study.com Gives useful tips for effective study.

www.kidshealth.org Provides study tips and helpful information on improving your study skills.

INDIVIDUAL ACTIVITY

Thinking creatively and critically

Take ten minutes to read and study the following text about healthy eating for teenage athletes. Then, on the next page, write down as many facts as you can remember. Use any study techniques that you think might help you.

FUEL YOUR BODY

As a teenage athlete, your active lifestyle and growing body means you have special nutritional needs. You need to start with the basics of a healthy and varied diet. There are no quick fixes. If you are playing sport or competing in athletics regularly for your school or a club, what you eat and drink is important in helping you to perform at your best. Good nutrition can help you by delaying fatigue and improving your skill and concentration. A healthy diet can also prevent injury and illness and help you achieve fitness and training targets. In contrast, poor nutrition can prevent you from achieving your training targets as it will increase your likelihood of injury, cause fatigue and decrease your concentration and skill.

IMPORTANT TIPS FOR A HEALTHY DIET

Try to organise food in advance as this can stop you eating unhealthy foods when you are tired and hungry. Eating a good breakfast every morning will help set you up for the day. Make sure to take in enough fluids; the recommended amount is eight glasses of water a day (milk, tea and other drinks can also be counted in this). Use healthy snacks to boost nutrition: sandwiches/rolls/pitta/bagels with cottage cheese, banana, salad, tuna, turkey, ham or chicken, natural yoghurt, cold boiled eggs, fresh fruit and nuts and dried fruit are all good options.

MUSCLE-BUILDING

Protein is needed for building and repairing muscle. Lean red meat, soya and tofu, chicken, turkey, nuts, fish, pulses, eggs, yoghurt, low-fat milk and cheese are all excellent sources of protein. Teenage athletes should include protein-rich foods at each main meal and after exercise to support muscle growth and repair. Carbohydrates also play an important part in gaining muscle. If you are not eating enough to meet your energy needs, then you won't be able to build or maintain muscle mass.

SNACKS BEFORE, DURING AND AFTER EXERCISE

BEFORE EXERCISE

To ensure your energy levels are at their best when you exercise, eat a meal or snack that is high in carbohydrates two to three hours before you exercise. Some ideas for pre-exercise snacks include: toast (add banana or nut butter as a topping); chicken with rice and salad; jacket potatoes with beans, tuna or chicken and salsa.

DURING EXERCISE

During tough training sessions or a competition lasting longer than sixty minutes, consider having an isotonic sports drink to replace fluids. For any training that lasts up to sixty minutes, water is fine.

AFTER EXERCISE

To restore your energy levels after exercise and to maintain muscle mass, eat a snack that is high in carbohydrates and protein. This could be mixed fruit salad with Greek yoghurt topped with mixed nuts and seeds. If you find it hard to eat after exercise, drinking semi-skimmed or skimmed milk is a good alternative. Timing can be important: aim to have a snack within the first 30–60 minutes after exercise and a meal a couple of hours after this.

SUPPLEMENTS

Supplements come in many forms – drinks, protein powders, shakes, bars, liquid meal replacements, creatine, caffeine, herbal preparations and more. Sports supplements have not been tested on teenagers or children so there is zero evidence to show that they are safe for a growing body. Sports supplements are therefore **not recommended** for anyone under 18 years of age. Supplements won't make you faster, stronger or more skilful. As a young person playing sport, your focus should be on developing a good nutritional foundation through eating a varied, balanced diet and timing your nutrition to fuel up and recover adequately.

(ADAPTED FROM WWW.SAFEFOOD.EU)

Facts I can remember

Study skills

Understanding how to prepare and get organised for school, homework and study is very important. It is also important to know *how* to study. We will look at three different ways of studying that can help you study and work more effectively:

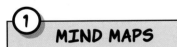 **MIND MAPS**

 **FLASH CARDS**

 **MNEMONICS**

 **MIND MAPS**

A mind map is a way of making study notes using colours, images and words to connect information on certain topics. Mind maps can help you to summarise, organise important ideas and recall information. Four easy steps for making a mind map are:

STEP 1	STEP 2	STEP 3	STEP 4
Use a highlighter to highlight important information in your notes or textbook.	Create an image or write a word that represents the main topic you are studying.	From that main idea, create branches (as many as needed) that represent words linked to the main topic. Each branch should have a single word (and possibly an image) that is related to the main word.	Create sub-branches from the main branches that expand on the words in the branches.

② FLASH CARDS

Flash cards can help you to summarise large amounts of information and to remember information such as important vocabulary, definitions and formulas, etc. There are three easy steps to creating good flashcards. Remember to write clearly. Using colours can also help you recall information, e.g. use green for notes on the past tense of verbs; use red for the future tense, etc.

STEP 1

Use a highlighter to highlight important information in your notes or textbook.

STEP 2

On one side of the flash card, write the main topic in large writing. On the other side of the card, write bullet points on the most important points of the topic. Do not write long sentences or detailed notes; use single words or short phrases.

STEP 3

If you want to expand on any of the bullet points, write that bullet point on one side of a new card and then write out the most important details about that bullet point in words and short phrases on the other side.

③ MNEMONICS

A mnemonic is a system or a way to remember something. You might remember from *My Wellbeing Journey 1* that the mnemonic for remembering the colours of the rainbow is **R**ichard **O**f **Y**ork **G**ave **B**attle **I**n **V**ain. Your teachers may give you mnemonics to help you in different areas like maths or English, e.g. a great way of remembering how to spell the word 'necessary' is 'One collar and two socks'. You can also come up with your own mnemonics to help you remember tricky spellings or formulas.

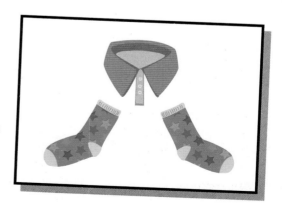

Let's use the different study techniques to study the 'Fuel your body' text.

Making a mind map

1. Read the text again and identify the main topic/subject.

2. Highlight the important points. (See the graphic on the next page for how this might be done.)

3. Write the main topic in the centre of your page.

4. Add branches with the important ideas around this topic.

5. Add sub-branches to give more detail on these ideas.

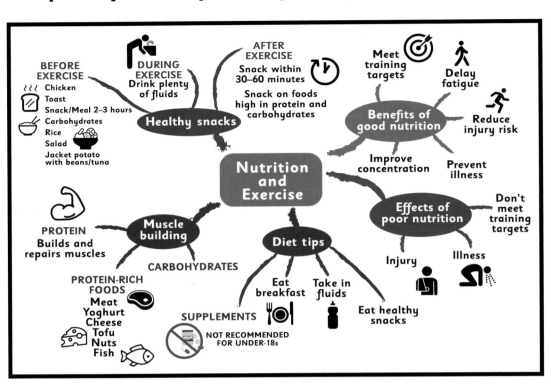

Making flashcards

Flashcards highlight the important information from the text.

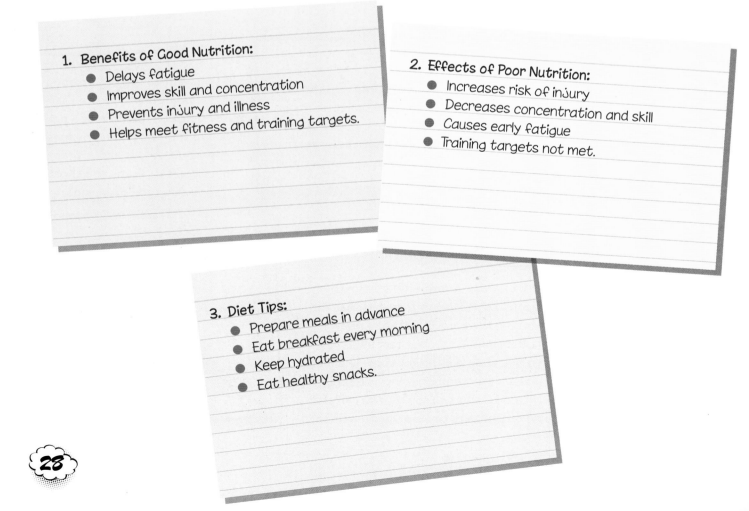

1. **Benefits of Good Nutrition:**
   - Delays fatigue
   - Improves skill and concentration
   - Prevents injury and illness
   - Helps meet fitness and training targets.

2. **Effects of Poor Nutrition:**
   - Increases risk of injury
   - Decreases concentration and skill
   - Causes early fatigue
   - Training targets not met.

3. **Diet Tips:**
   - Prepare meals in advance
   - Eat breakfast every morning
   - Keep hydrated
   - Eat healthy snacks.

4. Muscle-Building:
- Protein builds and prepares muscles
- Sources include lean red meat, soya and tofu, chicken, eggs, turkey and fish, nuts, pulses, eggs, yoghurt, low-fat milk and cheese
- Carbohydrates are also essential.

5. Supplements:
- Zero evidence to show they are safe
- Not recommended for under-18s.

6. Before, During and After Exercise:
- Eat carbohydrates 2–3 hours before exercise
- Keep hydrated with water during exercise
- Drink isotonic drinks if exercise lasts more than one hour
- After exercise eat a combination of carbohydrates and protein.

HIGHLIGHTING IMPORTANT INFORMATION IN AN ARTICLE

FUEL YOUR BODY

As a teenage athlete, your active lifestyle and growing body means you have special nutritional needs. You need to start with the basics of a healthy and varied diet. There are no quick fixes. If you are playing sport or competing in athletics regularly for your school or a club, what you eat and drink is important in helping you to perform at your best. Good nutrition can help you by delaying fatigue and improving your skill and concentration. A healthy diet can also prevent injury and illness and help you achieve fitness and training targets. In contrast, poor nutrition can prevent you from achieving your training targets as it will increase your likelihood of injury, cause fatigue and decrease your concentration and skill.

IMPORTANT TIPS FOR A HEALTHY DIET

Try to organise food in advance as this can stop you eating unhealthy foods when you are tired and hungry. Eating a good breakfast every morning will help set you up for the day. Make sure to take in enough fluids; the recommended amount is eight glasses of water a day (milk, tea and other drinks can also be counted in this). Use healthy snacks to boost nutrition: sandwiches/rolls/pitta/bagels with cottage cheese, banana, salad, tuna, turkey, ham or chicken, natural yoghurt, cold boiled eggs, fresh fruit and nuts and dried fruit are all good options.

MUSCLE-BUILDING

Protein is needed for building and repairing muscle. Lean red meat, soya and tofu, chicken, turkey, nuts, fish, pulses, eggs, yoghurt, low-fat milk and cheese are all excellent sources of protein. Teenage athletes should include protein-rich foods at each main meal and after

exercise to support muscle growth and repair. Carbohydrates also play an important part in gaining muscle. If you are not eating enough to meet your energy needs, then you won't be able to build or maintain muscle mass.

SNACKS BEFORE, DURING AND AFTER EXERCISE

BEFORE EXERCISE
To ensure your energy levels are at their best when you exercise, eat a meal or snack that is high in carbohydrates two to three hours before you exercise. Some ideas for pre-exercise snacks include: toast (add banana or nut butter as a topping); chicken with rice and salad; jacket potatoes with beans, tuna or chicken and salsa.

 DURING EXERCISE
During tough training sessions or a competition lasting longer than sixty minutes, consider having an isotonic sports drink to replace fluids. For any training that lasts up to sixty minutes, water is fine.

AFTER EXERCISE
To restore your energy levels after exercise and to maintain muscle mass, eat a snack that is high in carbohydrates and protein. This could be mixed fruit salad with Greek yoghurt topped with mixed nuts and seeds. If you find it hard to eat after exercise, drinking semi-skimmed or skimmed milk is a good alternative. Timing can be important: aim to have a snack within the first 30–60 minutes after exercise and a meal a couple of hours after this.

SUPPLEMENTS

Supplements come in many forms – drinks, protein powders, shakes, bars, liquid meal replacements, creatine, caffeine, herbal preparations and more. Sports supplements have not been tested on teenagers or children so there is zero evidence to show that they are safe for a growing body. Sports supplements are therefore **not recommended** for anyone under 18 years of age. Supplements won't make you faster, stronger or more skilful. As a young person playing sport, your focus should be on developing a good nutritional foundation through eating a varied, balanced diet and timing your nutrition to fuel up and recover adequately.

(ADAPTED FROM WWW.SAFEFOOD.EU)

Mnemonics

To help you remember important points from the text, e.g. good sources of protein, you can create a mnemonic. A good way to do this is to make a sentence where the first letter of each word is the first letter of each protein source. For example: *My young cousin Timmy can never find enough purple sweets.*

MNEMONIC	STUDY LIST
My	Meat
Young	Yoghurt
Cousin	Cheese
Timmy	Tofu
Can	Chicken
Never	Nuts
Find	Fish
Enough	Eggs
Purple	Pulses
Sweets	Soya

INDIVIDUAL ACTIVITY

Gathering, recording, organising and evaluating information and data

Choose a topic from a subject of your choice and apply the study skills you have just learned about in this lesson.

LEARNING KEEPSAKE

Three things I have learned in this lesson are:

1. _____

2. _____

3. _____

Something that helped me learn in this lesson was:

_____

_____

_____

As a result of this lesson, I will:

_____

_____

_____

_____ has shared this Learning Keepsake with me _____

Name of student   *Parent's/Guardian's signature*

Making Decisions

Learning outcomes: 1.6, 2.5

responsible   resilient   aware

By the end of this lesson you will:

→ have further developed your decision-making skills

KEYWORDS

Decision
Process
Consequences

Not all decisions have serious consequences, but there are some decisions in life that are difficult to make. Some of the choices we make can affect our lives long after we have made them.

Six decision-making styles

Here are six decision-making styles that young people often adopt.

1. **Looking at the advantages and disadvantages:** Carefully considering your options and the consequences of your actions, and then making your decision.

2. **Going along with everyone else:** Doing what everyone else is doing; following the crowd.

3. **Going with your gut feeling:** Making your decision based on how you feel.

4. **Asking for help:** Taking advice from somebody you trust.

5. **Acting on impulse:** Making a snap decision; acting without thinking.

6. **Biding your time:** Putting off making the decision for as long as possible; adopting a 'wait and see' approach.

Hey, I've got an opinion about this!

Listening and expressing myself

Being confident

PAIR ACTIVITY

In pairs, discuss and write down which **decision-making style** is most appropriate for each of the following decisions. Give reasons for your answers.

Will I wear the blue or the red top?

_____

_____

What subjects should I pick for my Leaving Certificate?

_____

_____

Will I drop to Ordinary Level Maths in Second Year?

_____

_____

Will I drink alcohol with my friends or not?

_____

_____

Will I tell my friend that our other friend is saying mean things about her behind her back?

_____

_____

Will I copy my homework from a friend or will I own up to not having done it?

_____

_____

Will I join the basketball team or the soccer team?

_____

_____

_____

I think my parents will still be out when I get home, so will I stay out with my friends an extra hour?

_____

_____

Will I go to the cinema with Sarah, as promised, or will I go to the school party?

_____

_____

_____

_____

ABCDE decision-making model

Sometimes we must make difficult decisions. It is good to have a strategy to help us do this. The following model can help you with making good decisions.

A >> **ASSESS** the problem

What decision has to be made?

B >> **BRAINSTORM** the solutions

List the different options you can choose.

C >> **CONSIDER** the consequences of each decision

What are the consequences of each of the choices you could make?

D >> **DECIDE** and act

Decide what you want to do.

E >> **EVALUATE** your decision

Analyse the pros and cons of your choice and reflect on your decision.

GROUP ACTIVITY

Discussing/
Debating

Making considered
decisions

Read the scenarios below and apply the ABCDE decision-making model to each case.

Scenario 1

Every month you go to the teenage disco with your friends. Your parents have allowed you to go because they trust you. Some of your friends usually go to the field near the disco to drink alcohol beforehand. You usually manage to avoid this, even though you get slagged off for not drinking. You have seen some bad fights break out at the disco after people have been drinking. Last month you saw at least four people passed out because of alcohol, and they had to be taken away by ambulance. You are a little curious about  alcohol but you are scared in case you have a bad reaction to it. This week your mother is dropping you to your friend's house before you go to the disco and you know you will find it hard to avoid going to the field with them before the disco.

A _____

B _____

C _____

D _____

E _____

Scenario 2

You have always loved sport. Your school basketball team has got through to the regional quarter-final, but it clashes with the semi-final of the Gaelic football championship. You are an important member of both teams and you have good friends on both. You are the top scorer on the basketball team and last time you scored the winning basket, but your parents love Gaelic football and go to all your matches, and your Gaelic football friends expect you to play in the semi-final.

A _____
_____
_____

B _____
_____
_____

C _____
_____
_____

D _____
_____
_____

E _____
_____
_____

INDIVIDUAL ACTIVITY

Making considered
decisions

Now apply the ABCDE model to a problem you have to or had to solve in your own life. Use the steps from the ABCDE model to help you.

A Assess the problem and decide what decision has to be made.

_____

_____

_____

B Brainstorm the solutions: what are the different options you could choose?

_____

_____

_____

C Consider the consequences of each decision: what are the consequences of each possible choice for your future?

_____

_____

_____

D Decide and act: decide what you want to do.

_____

_____

_____

E Evaluate your decision: analyse the pros and cons of your choice and reflect on your decision.

_____

_____

_____

LEARNING KEEPSAKE

Three things I have learned in this lesson are:

1. _____

2. _____

3. _____

Something that helped me learn in this lesson was:

_____

_____

_____

As a result of this lesson, I will:

_____

_____

_____

_____ has shared this Learning Keepsake with me _____

Name of student   *Parent's/Guardian's signature*

LESSON 7

Feeling Unwell

Learning outcome: 1.7

responsible   resilient   aware

By the end of this lesson you will:

↪ be able to recognise the symptoms of common illnesses

↪ be able to identify the causes of these illnesses

↪ recognise the importance of good hygiene in preventing illness or disease

KEYWORDS

Disease

Illness

Symptoms

USEFUL WEBSITES

www.safefood.eu Offers useful tips on food hygiene.

www.hse.ie Search 'Conditions and treatments' for the A–Z about hundreds of medical conditions and treatments.

A healthy lifestyle can help us to stay fit and healthy and to ward off illness. However, it is inevitable that we will pick up illnesses from time to time. In this lesson you will learn about common illnesses and their symptoms. You will also learn how you can help prevent the spread of these illnesses.

INDIVIDUAL ACTIVITY

Evaluating information and data

The cards below show different illnesses or conditions, their symptoms and treatments. In the table, match each illness card to its symptoms and identify the correct treatment. The first one has been done for you.

ILLNESSES/CONDITIONS

A Common cold **B** Head lice **C** Athlete's foot

D Warts **E** Food poisoning **F** Cold sores

vi Over-the-counter anti-viral creams. Only effective if applied at the first sign of infection.
TREATMENT

iii Usually clear up without treatment. They can also be removed by a GP.
TREATMENT

iv Hydration – drink at least two litres of water per day, as well as an extra 200 ml of water every time you pass diarrhoea. Eat easily digestible food such as toast. If symptoms persist, contact your GP.
TREATMENT

3 Small, blister-like lesions that usually appear in and around the mouth. Caused by the herpes virus. Once someone has been exposed to the virus, it lies dormant in their system and can come back again.
SYMPTOMS

5 Sneezing; stuffy, runny nose; coughing; hoarseness; general feeling of being unwell.
SYMPTOMS

6 Itchy scalp (but not in all cases so a close inspection is necessary). A rash may also appear on the back of the neck.
SYMPTOMS

ii Plenty of fluids; rest; healthy diet. Steam inhalation (holding your head over a bowl of hot water, with a towel over your head). Decongestants.
TREATMENT

v Anti-fungal creams and sprays available from your pharmacy.
TREATMENT

i Wet combing with a special fine-tooth available from pharmacies. Repeat the procedure on days 5, 9 and 13.
TREATMENT

4 Several different types. Tiny infections on the skin caused by a virus. They appear round and oval, firm and raised, with a cauliflower-like appearance. Most common on the knuckles, fingers and knees.
SYMPTOMS

1 Caused by eating food that has been contaminated with bacteria. Symptoms usually develop after one to three days. The most common symptoms are nausea, vomiting, cramp and diarrhoea.
SYMPTOMS

2 Caused by a fungal infection. It appears as a rash between the toes, causing the skin to become itchy, scaly, flaky, dry and red. There may also be a burning or stinging sensation.
SYMPTOMS

CONDITION	SYMPTOM	TREATMENT
A	5	ii
B		
C		
D		
E		
F		

39

Preventing common illnesses and minimising the risk or spread of infection

Often, common illnesses cannot be avoided but we can minimise the spread of infections.

Common cold

- Wash your hands regularly and properly, particularly after touching your nose or mouth and before handling food.
- Always sneeze and cough into a tissue. Throw away used tissues and wash your hands.
- Clean surfaces regularly to keep them free from germs.
- Use your own cup, plate, cutlery and kitchen utensils.
- Do not share towels or washcloths.

Head lice

A head lice infestation cannot be easily prevented. Regular wet combing with a fine-toothed comb is the best way to find new lice quickly. To prevent the spread of head lice:

- avoid sharing combs and brushes
- avoid activities that lead to head-to-head contact
- keep belongings, especially upper body clothing, away from shared areas like coat closets

Athlete's foot

The best way to prevent athlete's foot is to practise good foot hygiene.

- Wash your feet and between your toes daily.
- Take care to dry between your toes after showering and bathing.
- Avoid tight-fitting footwear, especially during the summer.
- Do not put on socks, tights or stockings before your feet are completely dry.
- When using communal changing rooms or shower areas, wear flip-flops or plastic sandals, where possible.
- Alternating footwear can ensure that shoes are dry at all times.
- Avoid borrowing shoes.

Warts

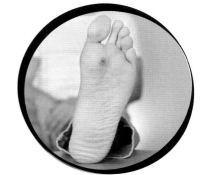

- Do not touch other people's warts.
- Do not share towels.
- Avoid scratching or picking a wart as this will cause it to spread.

Cold sores

- Avoid touching your cold sore unless you are applying a cream.

- Always wash your hands before and after applying cream and after touching the affected area.

- Do not share creams or medication with other people as this can cause the infection to spread.

- Do not share items that come into contact with the affected area such as lipsticks or cutlery.

- Avoid kissing.

- If you have a cold sore, be particularly careful around pregnant women, newborn babies and people with weak immune systems.

Being healthy

The picture below shows a kitchen displaying a number of food safety hazards. In pairs, look at the picture carefully. Mark with an X the things that you think are hazardous and/or could contribute to cases of food poisoning.

Preventing food poisoning

A useful way of preventing food poisoning is to remember the **4 Cs**:

1. CLEANING | **2. COOKING** | **3. CHILLING** | **4. CROSS-CONTAMINATION**

1. CLEANING

You can prevent the spread of harmful bacteria and viruses by having good personal hygiene and by keeping all your work surfaces and utensils clean. Wash your hands frequently with soap and water, particularly:

- after going to the toilet
- after rubbing a pet
- after handling raw food
- before preparing food

Bacteria: Tiny, single-celled organisms. Some can cause illness and disease, while others are good for you!

2. COOKING

- It is always important to cook food thoroughly, especially meat, as raw meat contains harmful bacteria. Make sure the food is piping hot in the middle.
- Some meat, such as steaks and joints of beef or lamb, can be served rare (not cooked in the middle) so long as the outside has been cooked properly.
- Do not reheat food more than once.

3. CHILLING

- It is important to keep foods at the correct temperature. Refrigerated food needs to be kept at 0–5°C (32–41°F).
- Do not leave food that needs to be chilled standing at room temperature.
- Do not put hot food in the fridge or freezer. Cooked leftovers should be cooled quickly, ideally within one to two hours, before being refrigerated or frozen.

4. CROSS-CONTAMINATION

Cross-contamination occurs when bacteria are transferred from foods (usually raw food) to other foods. To prevent cross-contamination:

- Always wash your hands after handling raw foods.
- Store and prepare raw foods separately from ready-to-eat foods.
- Store raw meat in sealable containers at the bottom of your fridge so it cannot drip onto other foods.
- Use different chopping boards for raw foods and ready-to-eat foods.
- Clean all utensils thoroughly after they have been used to cut/prepare raw foods.
- Never wash raw meat because harmful bacteria can be splashed around the sink and surrounding counter area.

Reading for enjoyment and with understanding

Being safe

PAIR ACTIVITY

In pairs, read about what Charlie does when he comes home from work. Identify his risky food and hygiene behaviour. Discuss the problems this behaviour can cause Charlie and what Charlie could do to prevent these risks.

Charlie comes home from a long day at work. He is tired and hungry. As soon as he opens the door, his dog, Cas, meets him, jumping with excitement. Charlie pats Cas hello. He then starts to prepare dinner.

On the counter top he finds yesterday's leftover rice, which he will use for dinner today. He sticks it in the microwave to heat it up. Opening the fridge, he spies a raw chicken and some carrots underneath. Liquid from the chicken seems to have dripped onto the carrots. Charlie wipes the spill off with his hand. He then takes the chicken over to the sink and washes it under the tap. He cuts it up using a knife and board he found in the sink, and puts the chicken into a frying pan.

Using the same board and knife, he chops the carrots, popping one or two in his mouth as he does so. He puts them on to boil, and he turns the microwave on again to reheat the rice. As the chicken is frying, Charlie tastes some to check if it is ready. He notices that the chicken is still raw in the centre but he is so hungry that he eats it anyway.

After dinner, Charlie has a shower. He realises that he forgot to bring in a clean towel so he reuses one that is lying on the bathroom floor. Charlie is in a hurry to bring his dog for a walk so he dries himself quickly, gets dressed and puts on his socks and walking shoes even though his feet are still a bit wet.

RISKY BEHAVIOUR	POSSIBLE RISKS	WAYS TO PREVENT POSSIBLE RISKS

LEARNING KEEPSAKE

Three things I have learned in this lesson are:

1. _____

2. _____

3. _____

Something that helped me learn in this lesson was:

_____

_____

_____

As a result of this lesson, I will:

_____

_____

_____

_____ has shared this Learning Keepsake with me _____

Name of student   *Parent's/Guardian's signature*

Water Safety

Learning outcomes: 1.6, 1.7

 responsible

 resilient

 aware

By the end of this lesson you will:

➜ know how to keep safe while swimming

 KEYWORDS

Difficulty

Parallel

Safety equipment

USEFUL WEBSITES

www.iws.ie Provides information about water safety.

www.respectthewater.com Provides information on survival techniques.

WATER SAFETY

Did you know that, on average, 133 people drown in Ireland each year? Many of these drownings occur in rivers and lakes, where it can be difficult to see or to determine how deep the water is. In Ireland, thirty children aged fourteen and under have drowned in the last ten years – the equivalent of an entire classroom. Many of these deaths were preventable. It is important to remember that every stretch of open water (beaches, ponds, rivers and lakes) has its own dangers and we should make ourselves aware of these dangers and learn the skills of safe swimming.

INDIVIDUAL ACTIVITY

Being safe

Each of the cartoons below has an important message about safe swimming. Match each cartoon with the relevant safety message. Then, in pairs, give one reason for each message.

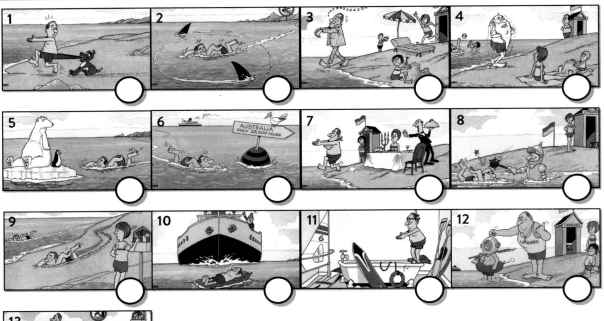

A. Don't swim alone.

B. Don't be a bully.

C. Pay attention to signs on the beach.

D. Swim parallel and close to the shore.

E. Don't stay in the water too long.

F. Never use air mattresses.

G. Don't swim out to sea.

H. Don't swim just after eating.

I. Don't swim in strange places.

J. Don't swim if you are feeling tired.

K. Don't swim out after anything drifting.

L. Obey the lifeguard.

M. Learn to use equipment before trying it out.

The Water Safety Code

Before swimming, it is important to consider the following four points:

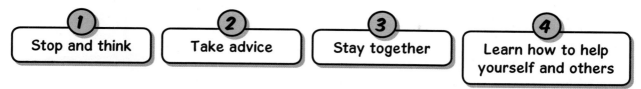

1 Stop and think   **2** Take advice   **3** Stay together   **4** Learn how to help yourself and others

 1   Stop and think

Every stretch of open water has its own set of dangers. When visiting an area of open water for the first time, take a few moments to look for any potential dangers. Ask yourself the following questions:

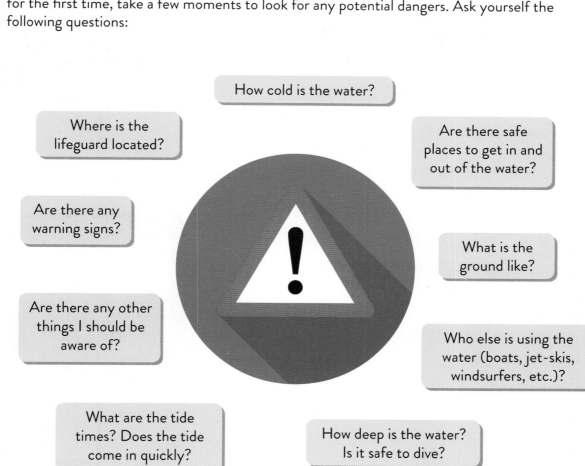

How cold is the water?

Where is the lifeguard located?

Are there safe places to get in and out of the water?

Are there any warning signs?

What is the ground like?

Are there any other things I should be aware of?

Who else is using the water (boats, jet-skis, windsurfers, etc.)?

What are the tide times? Does the tide come in quickly?

How deep is the water? Is it safe to dive?

Why are these safety messages important?

_____

_____

2   Take advice

Most beaches will have lifeguards on duty. If you are unsure of the area, ask the lifeguard about possible dangers. In addition to the dangers listed above, Irish Water Safety gives the following advice:

(i) Don't go tombstoning

Tombstoning is the name given to jumping into water from a height. It is a very dangerous, high-risk activity, which unfortunately has gained popularity among young people in recent years. Irish Water Safety strongly advises against it as incidences of it have led to serious injury and death. It is dangerous because:

○ Water depth alters with tide – it might be shallower than you think.

○ Submerged objects, such as rocks, may not be visible.

○ The water can be extremely cold, resulting in shock, which makes it difficult to swim.

○ There may be strong currents that can sweep you out to sea.

(ii) Be aware of rip currents

Rips are strong currents that can quickly take swimmers from shallow water out beyond their depth. Lifeguards will indicate where rips are so that you can avoid them, but if you do get caught in one:

○ Stay calm – don't panic.

○ If you can stand, wade rather than swim.

○ If you cannot wade, then float. Knowing how to float is an important survival skill, which we will discuss in more detail. If you have one, keep hold of your board or inflatable to help you float.

○ Raise your hand and shout for help.

○ Never try to swim directly against the rip – you will become exhausted.

○ Swim parallel to the beach until free of the rip, then make for shore.

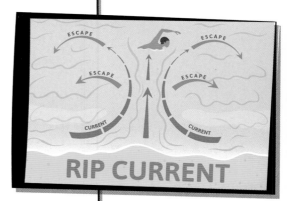

(iii) Avoid cold-water shock

Cold-water shock is a major contributing factor to drowning in Ireland as it causes the instinctive reaction to gasp uncontrollably. This can cause the person to breathe in water, which can lead to drowning. The shock can also lead to cardiac arrests or strokes. If you fall into cold water, fight the urge to thrash around; instead, try to calm yourself and float on your back. In about one minute to ninety seconds your body will become acclimatised to the cold and you will be able to reclaim control of your breathing. You'll also be able to think straight and plan your next move. You can practise floating the next time you're in the pool.

▶ **YouTube**

Go to YouTube and look up 'How to survive cold-water shock' (0:59) to see an RNLI video on the subject.

(iv) Know your flags

Do you know what the flags flown at beaches represent? Write down what you think each one means. (You'll find the answers at the bottom of the next page.)

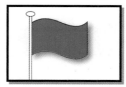

_____

_____

_____

_____

_____

_____

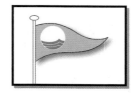

_____

_____

(v) Safe swimming for rivers and inland waters

○ Check where the ringbuoys are placed – they could save your life or someone else's. Report missing, stolen or vandalised ringbuoys to Irish Water Safety via its website **www.ringbuoys.ie**.

○ Never wade into a river to retrieve an item that has fallen in.

○ Do not jump off bridges – even if you see friends doing it.

○ Never push a friend into the water 'for a laugh'.

○ Be careful of slippery grass by the water's edge.

○ Watch out for tripping hazards near the water's edge.

○ Never swim in fast-flowing water. If you feel that it's dangerous, then do not swim – even if your friends say it's ok. If you are caught in a current, float on your back and travel downstream feet first to protect you head.

○ Beware of submerged objects – they can be very dangerous. Always enter the water feet first.

○ Do not play near the edge of overhanging riverbanks as they can crumble away unexpectedly from under you.

Why are these safety messages important?

_____

_____

3 Stay together

Never swim on your own. Always take someone with you (preferably an adult) and tell an adult where you plan to go.

Why is this safety message important?

_____

_____

4 Learn how to get help yourself and others

If you get into difficulty:

The Royal National Lifeboat Institution has developed the **'Float to Live'** campaign to save lives. This campaign gives some simple steps to follow if you find yourself in difficulty in cold water.

Five steps to float

1. Fight your instinct to thrash around.
2. Lean back and extend your arms and legs.
3. If you need to, gently move them around to help you float.
4. Float until you can control your breathing.
5. Only then, call for help and swim to safety.

(Source: www.respectthewater.com)

FLOAT FOR YOUR LIFE

If you fall into water, fight your instinct to swim until the cold water shock passes | FLOAT TO LIVE

Why is this safety message important?

_____

_____

_____

 **YouTube**

Go to YouTube and look up 'Float to Live: Evan's story' (2:30) to see how Evan used the message of the 'Float to Live' campaign to survive a rip current.

Red flag: No swimming allowed at all **Red and yellow flag:** Lifeguard on duty/Safe to swim between these flags **Black and white flag:** No swimming – area used by surfers and windsurfers **Blue flag:** Flag awarded to beaches with high water quality

If others get into difficulty:

At the beach

Never attempt a rescue. Tell a lifeguard, or if you can't see a lifeguard, call 999 or 112 and ask for the coast guard.

Rivers or inland water

Call 999 or 112 for the coast guard immediately. Shout to the person in difficulty and encourage them to shore. This will help orientate them. Reach out with a long object such as a branch or piece of clothing, and take care not to lean in too far. If one is available, throw a ringbuoy to the person, or any other floating object that might be to hand. Do not enter the water yourself. You can be of most help if you stay securely on the land.

Check out **www.iws.ie** for more useful information on keeping safe while swimming.

Protecting yourself from the sun

As well as all this, it is important to remember to protect yourself when sunbathing. Use a high-factor sunscreen, and always avoid direct exposure to the sun during the hottest part of the day, taking advantage of shade where you can. Remember:

Slip on a T-shirt.

Slop on some sunscreen.

Slap on a hat.

 INDIVIDUAL ACTIVITY

Being safe

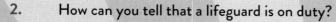

1. Check how much you have learned in today's lesson. Write the letter of the correct answer in each instance in the box.

   Water Safety Quiz

   1. When you get to a swimming area, what is the first thing you should do?

      (a) Stop and think

      (b) Look for the ice-cream shop

      (c) Go for a swim

   2. How can you tell that a lifeguard is on duty?

      (a) They always stand in the middle of the beach

      (b) There are yellow and red flags to tell you

      (c) They come over to you to tell you

3. What should you do if you see someone in trouble in the water?

(a) Dive in and rescue them

(b) Call for help

(c) Run away

4. What should you do before you dive?

(a) Make sure you are wearing your goggles

(b) Make sure the water is deep enough

(c) Make sure everyone can see your fantastic diving skills

5. If you find yourself in a rip current, the first thing to do is:

(a) Swim against the current

(b) Shout for help and wave both arms

(c) Stay calm – don't panic

6. If you find yourself suddenly in cold water, you should:

(a) Start swimming as hard as you can

(b) Raise your hands immediately to attract some help

(c) Stay calm and fight your instinct to thrash around

2. Now choose a common outdoor swimming site, whether it is the sea, a river or a lake. Using what you have learned in class today, along with doing some further research of your own on the Irish Water Safety website (www.iws.ie), design a billboard advertisement that raises awareness about safe swimming in that area.

LEARNING KEEPSAKE

Three things I have learned in this lesson are:

1. _____

2. _____

3. _____

Something that helped me learn in this lesson was:

_____

_____

_____

As a result of this lesson, I will:

_____

_____

_____

_____ has shared this Learning Keepsake with me _____

Name of student   *Parent's/Guardian's signature*

LESSON 9

Accidents at Home and at School

Learning outcome: 1.7

responsible   aware

By the end of this lesson you will:

➜ have a greater awareness of how to stay safe at home and at school

KEYWORDS

Accident

Prevention

Emergency

USEFUL WEBSITE

www.redcross.ie Provides information on first aid training.

Listening and expressing myself   Being safe

GROUP ACTIVITY

As a group, discuss and write down the different accidents that have happened to you or someone you know.

Evaluating information and data

PAIR ACTIVITY

In pairs, look at the images below. For each, list what accidents or injuries could occur and suggest how they can be avoided.

Possible dangers:
_____

Could be avoided:
_____
_____

Possible dangers:
_____

Could be avoided:
_____
_____

Possible dangers:
_____

Could be avoided:
_____
_____

Possible dangers:
_____

Could be avoided:
_____
_____

Possible dangers:
_____

Could be avoided:
_____
_____

Possible dangers:
_____

Could be avoided:
_____
_____

Possible dangers: _____

Could be avoided: _____

_____

_____

Possible dangers: _____

Could be avoided: _____

_____

_____

Possible dangers: _____

Could be avoided: _____

_____

_____

Being safe

Listening and expressing myself

GROUP ACTIVITY

Working as a group, come up with and then write down five tips to make your home and school a safer place.

HOME	SCHOOL
1	1
2	2
3	3
4	4
5	5

Personal safety

To prevent accidents happening, possible risks and safety hazards must be identified and removed. It is important to take responsibility for your environment and your behaviour to reduce the risk of accident and injury to yourself and others. It is also important to know how to treat minor injuries that may occur.

Burns

There are three types of burn:

1. First-degree burns: only the top layer of the skin is damaged. These burns are caused by brief contact with heat.

2. Second-degree burns: the damage is deeper and usually causes blisters and redness.

3. Third-degree burns: very deep burns. While they may be painless initially, they may need to be treated with skin grafts.

Treatment

Anyone who suffers a second- or third-degree burn should go to a hospital straight away. If someone has a first-degree burn (or a second-degree burn and you cannot get them to hospital immediately), follow these steps:

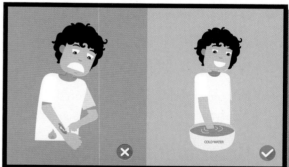

- Remove any clothing from around the area, but do not remove any clothing that is stuck to the skin.

- Run cool water over the burn for about ten minutes.

- Remove rings or watches, which may be difficult to remove if the area becomes swollen later.

- Apply a gauze bandage.

Do not:

- break blisters

- apply lotions, creams or ointments to large burn areas

Poisons

Treatment

If you suspect someone has taken a poison and they are still conscious, you should:

- Stay calm and act quickly.

- Seek medical advice as soon as possible.

- Find out as much as possible about the poison they have taken.

- Call the Poisons Information Centre on (01) 809 2166 (8 a.m.–10 p.m.).

- Always take the product container with you when speaking on the telephone or to the GP or hospital.

- Bring a sample of the poison or the vomit to the hospital.
- If a chemical has splashed into the eyes, wash the eyes with tap water for 15 minutes.
- Wash any skin that was in contact with the poison with soap and water.

Do not:

- make the person vomit

Nosebleeds

Treatment

- Put on gloves.
- Lean the person's head forward.
- Pinch or get the person to pinch the soft part of their nose.
- Apply pressure for about 10 minutes.
- Advise the patient to breathe through their mouth.
- Seek medical advice if bleeding occurs for longer than 30 minutes or if bleeding recurs.

Do not:

- tilt your head back
- blow your nose – and don't blow your nose for some hours

Sprains and strains

Treatment

- Remember RICE:

R – Rest. Rest the injured muscle.

I – Ice. Apply a cold compress for 20 minutes and keep reapplying: this helps to reduce swelling.

C – Compression. Apply a firm bandage to reduce swelling.

E – Elevate. Raise the injured area to reduce blood flow.

Fractures

Treatment

- Stop any bleeding by elevating the affected area and applying pressure to the wound using sterile bandages.

- Immobilise the injured area.

- Apply ice to the injured area.

- Treat the person for shock by getting them into a comfortable position and keeping them warm with a blanket.

- Call the emergency services on 999 or 112.

Note that if you are unsure whether the injury is a sprain/strain or a fracture, you should treat it as a fracture.

Fainting

Fainting occurs when there is a lack of blood reaching the brain.

Treatment

If someone is feeling faint:

- Get them to sit down and place their head between their knees.

- Tell them to take deep breaths.

- Allow them to sit up slowly.

- Offer sips of water.

- Alternatively, get the person to lie down with their legs raised.

Cuts and wounds

Most cuts can be easily treated at home, but you should seek medical advice for deeper cuts and wounds that do not stop bleeding.

For minor cuts:

- Put on gloves.

- If the cut is dirty, clean it with a sterile wipe or run water over it.

- If there is a lot of bleeding, apply pressure to the wound until the bleeding stops.

- Raise the wounded area where necessary.

- Dress the affected area with a sterile pad and bandage.

First aid is the first treatment given to a person who has been injured or taken ill. A basic knowledge of first aid can be very helpful. There are many courses available throughout Ireland – why not find out about one in your area?

Learning with others

In pairs, practise some of the treatments for the minor injuries listed above.

LEARNING KEEPSAKE

Three things I have learned in this lesson are:

1. _____

2. _____

3. _____

Something that helped me learn in this lesson was:

_____

_____

_____

As a result of this lesson, I will:

_____

_____

_____

_____ has shared this Learning Keepsake with me _____

Name of student *Parent's/Guardian's signature*

LESSON 10

Respecting My Privacy – My Digital Footprint

Learning outcome: 1.7

responsible   resilient   aware

By the end of this lesson you will:

→ understand the concept of privacy and how your own privacy can be compromised

→ appreciate the importance of privacy in your online interactions

KEYWORDS

Privacy

Digital footprint

USEFUL WEBSITES

www.kidshealth.org Provides information and tips on internet safety.

www.childnet.com Provides tips, blogs and advice on how to use the internet safely, responsibly and positively.

PRIVACY ONLINE

While we are now more aware of the dangers of sharing information online, we still don't fully realise the extent to which our increasing use of technology will impact our privacy. It is important to realise that everything we do online can never be fully deleted. This can leave a trail that can allow people to use this information for their own purpose. As a child, your parents warned you against talking to strangers to protect your personal safety. Now, as a young adult becoming aware of your personal safety, you should be wary about sharing private information with strangers. You wouldn't share personal information with a stranger you pass on the street, yet many people think that it is OK to post private information online for everyone to see. Modern technology can distance us from reality and it is important to realise that our online actions have consequences.

GROUP ACTIVITY

Being responsible, safe and ethical
in using digital technology

In groups, brainstorm what you understand by the term 'online privacy'.

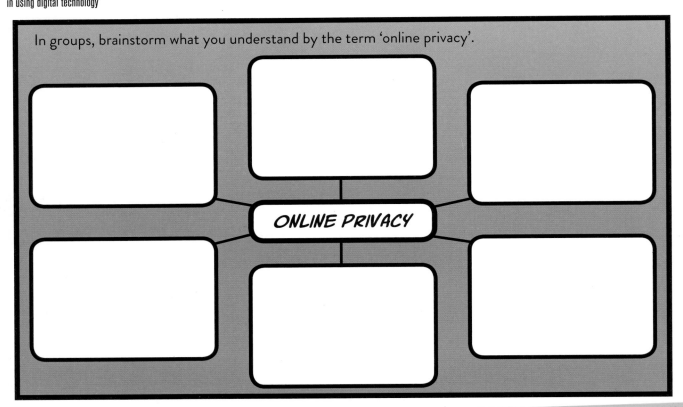

ONLINE PRIVACY

CLASS DISCUSSION

Discussing/Debating

Below are some celebrities or public figures you more than likely recognise.

Can you name these people?

What are the positive and negative effects of being in the public eye?

Why do you think you know these people?

Are their lives private?

INDIVIDUAL ACTIVITY

Being responsible, safe and ethical
in using digital technology

On the screen below, give examples of what you share online (e.g. pictures you post, comments you make). Think about your social media profile, blog posts, YouTube videos, and any other information you share online.

GROUP ACTIVITY

Being responsible, safe and ethical
in using digital technology

In groups, discuss and then write down the advantages and disadvantages of using social media.

ADVANTAGES	DISADVANTAGES

Leaving a trail: Our digital footprint

Our digital footprint is the term used to describe the trail, traces or footprints we leave, knowingly or unknowingly, every time we go online. Every time you search a website, post online, send a text or email, or visit a social network, you are adding to your digital footprint. Our digital footprint paints a picture of who we are so it's important to realise what kind of trail we are leaving and what the possible effects can be.

Unlike the footprints we leave in the sand, which are temporary, digital footprints are permanent.

Tips for protecting our digital footprint

☛ **Think before you send:** Your digital profile is your online portrait and can paint a positive or negative impression of you and your behaviour. Be conscious of painting a good picture. Count to ten before you send anything. Ask yourself if you would be comfortable with your family, teachers or future employers seeing these messages or images now or in twenty years' time. Remember these rules:

   ☛ The granny rule: Would you be happy with your granny seeing this information about you?

   ☛ The T-shirt rule: Would you put what you're going to post on a T-shirt and wear it all day?

☛ **Remember 'It's permanent!':** It can be very easy to get caught up in the excitement of sharing things with friends through social media, but it is important to remember that nothing can be permanently deleted in the online world. Anything shared online is not private. It can be copied and shared very quickly by any number of people. Even if you take it down, it's still out there.

☛ **Safeguard your private information:** Private information such as passwords, PIN numbers, addresses, phone numbers or personal details should never be shared online as they can be used by others for their own personal gain or to bring you harm. Strong, secure passwords are important. Choose one that could not be easily guessed and change it often. If someone knows your password, they can gain access to all your private information and, even worse, steal your identity.

☞ **Check your privacy settings:** If you don't want the whole world to see your social media profile, then you must check each site's privacy guidelines and take the necessary steps to keep your profile as private as possible.

☞ **Don't respond to unknown messages or emails:** Don't accept or respond to messages, files or emails from people you don't know. Many unsolicited (you didn't sign up for them) messages are simply scams to trick you into giving personal information or money. Not everything you read or every person you meet online is genuine. If you receive any online messages that make you feel nervous, worried or uncomfortable, be sure to inform a trusted adult.

☞ **Think about future employers:** It is common practice for employers to research employees via their social networking platforms. What they see there can influence the perception they have of you and could be a factor in them deciding whether or not you get the job. Before you post, think about what impression you want your digital footprint to give to future employers.

☞ **Watch out for targeted advertising:** Private companies, social media companies and marketing agencies can track your online movements across websites. This allows them to build a profile of you and your habits so they can then send advertisements and other messages directly to you that they know will interest you. For example, if you are browsing for shoes online, the next time you are on a social media site you will most likely receive multiple adverts for all types of shoes. Stricter rules about how companies collect, store, process and share personal information require them to seek your consent to do this and inform you in their 'Privacy Statement'. However, you should always carefully consider what information you voluntarily share.

GDPR – General Data Protection Regulation

In May 2018, a major piece of law was introduced across the EU to make companies more open and accountable for the information that they collect about individuals and how it is used. It offers individuals increased rights in terms of accessing and understanding what information is held about them.

Being responsible, safe and ethical
in using digital technology

INDIVIDUAL ACTIVITY

1. Answer the questions about your digital footprint. For each 'Yes' answer you give, colour in the corresponding number on the footprint diagram. If you answer 'No', leave the corresponding foot section blank. On each of the toes, write in the names of the social media platforms you use, e.g. Instagram, Snapchat, WhatsApp.

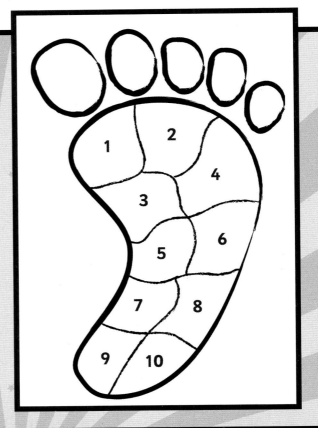

QUESTIONS	YES	NO
1. Have you ever given your personal details online (e.g. phone number, email address, street address, etc.)?		
2. Have you ever posted or shared secrets or embarrassing information about yourself?		
3. Are there photos of you online?		
4. Do you share information with people online you don't really know?		
5. Have you ever added people to your friends list who you have never met face to face?		
6. Do you purchase goods online?		
7. Have you ever commented on other posts online?		
8. Have you ever posted things on social media that you later regretted?		
9. Have you posted online something you would not say in real life?		
10. Has someone posted a picture of you online without your permission?		

2. What do you think your digital footprint says about you?

_____

_____

LEARNING KEEPSAKE

Three things I have learned in this lesson are:

1. _____

2. _____

3. _____

Something that helped me learn in this lesson was:

_____

_____

_____

As a result of this lesson, I will:

_____

_____

_____

_____ has shared this Learning Keepsake with me _____

Name of student   *Parent's/Guardian's signature*

MEET THE CHALLENGE

Strand 1 Topic 3

1. A VIDEO ON STUDY TIPS

Learning outcomes: 1.5, 4.8

Go to YouTube and look up 'The 9 Best Scientific Study Tips' (AsapSCIENCE, 3:25). Working in groups, make your own short video on study tips for young people.

○ Plan your content.

○ Include information on:

· study techniques

· time management

· exam preparation

· goal-setting

○ Include any other information your group feels is relevant.

○ Include images and diagrams to make your video more appealing to viewers.

Your video could then be uploaded to the school website!

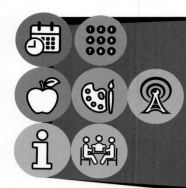

MEET THE CHALLENGE

Strand 1 Topic 3
2. 'STAY SAFE ONLINE' CAMPAIGN

Learning outcomes: 1.1, 1.6

Your class has decided to organise a campaign to raise awareness in your school on how to stay safe online and how to create a more positive digital footprint. For this campaign, your class will divide up into four groups, with each group running a different aspect of the campaign.

○ **Group 1: Poster group**

This group will create posters highlighting the importance of staying safe online, including tips on how to stay safe and how to create a positive digital footprint. The posters will be displayed in different areas around the school.

○ **Group 2: Information leaflet group**

This group will create an information leaflet to be distributed to students in the school informing them on how they can stay safe online and how they can create a positive digital footprint.

○ **Group 3: Presentation group**

This group will plan and deliver a presentation to different classes in the school on the topic of staying safe online and creating a positive digital footprint.

○ **Group 4: School website/social media group**

This group will design a page for the school website and other school social media accounts on online safety and creating a positive digital footprint.

○ Each group should include the following in their part of the campaign:

· information on social media and common social media sites/apps used by young people

· what a digital footprint is and how to create a positive one

· how social media can be dangerous

· tips on how to stay safe online

· tips on how to create a positive digital footprint

· catchy slogans and pictures

· any other information your group thinks is relevant

TOPIC 4
My Rights and the Rights of Others

responsible · connected · respected · aware

By the end of this lesson you will:

➡ have examined the different relationships in your family

➡ appreciate that all families have similarities and differences

➡ examine conflict in family life and understand how to deal with it

KEYWORDS

Relationships
Family
Conflict
Expectations
Roles

GROUP ACTIVITY

Learning with others

1. In groups, brainstorm what the word 'family' means to your group.

FAMILY

2. As a group, identify and write down what you think are the different family types depicted in the image. Can you think of other types of families that are not shown.

_____

_____

_____

_____

_____

_____

_____

Learning creatively

CLASS ACTIVITY

Your teacher will choose four people to role-play the following family drama.

Family Life

It is Tuesday morning in the Murphy household and the family is getting ready for school and for work.

Mrs Murphy *(shouting up the stairs)*: Eoin, it's ten to eight – are you out of bed yet?

Eoin *(shouting from his bedroom)*: I'm waiting for Brid to get out of the bathroom so I can have a shower.

Mrs Murphy: Well, come down and eat your breakfast while you're waiting; we don't have that much time left.

Eoin comes downs the stairs to the kitchen to have his breakfast.

Brid *(shouting to her mother from the bathroom)*: Is my hockey gear ready? I've a match today.

Mrs Murphy: I don't know; I told you to get it organised last night.

Mr Murphy *(passing Brid on the stairs)*: What are you doing with all that make-up on and those earrings going to school? I thought we talked about this?

Brid: Oh, Dad, relax. Everyone in school wears them. I don't have time to take them off now anyway, we're in a hurry.

Mrs Murphy: Eoin, where are you going? Sit down and finish your cereal. And have you packed your lunch?

Eoin: I still have to have a shower.

Mr Murphy: I thought we'd agreed you'd make your own lunches every night, Eoin. Your mother has enough to do.

Eoin: But, Dad, I had training until six last night and then I had after-school study until ten – I was wrecked when I got home. Can I have a fiver for a roll instead?

Mrs Murphy: I'll make you a sandwich this time, Eoin, but you'll have to be more organised tomorrow. We're not wasting our money on rolls.

Eoin: Can I have two euros to get something before study so? I'm always starving after training.

Mr Murphy: No! Bring an extra sandwich. Now hurry up because I have to leave on time this morning – I don't want to get stuck in traffic.

Brid: I need two euros for the bus to the hockey match.

Mr Murphy: Here *(handing Brid the money)*. Now, good luck in the match. I'll text you later to see how you got on.

Eoin: Hey! That's not fair! How come she gets two euros and I don't?

Learning with others

As a group, discuss and then answer these questions.

1. Make a list of the different sources of conflict in the Murphy household.

_____

_____

_____

2. Make a list of other issues that can cause conflict in families.

_____

_____

_____

3. Pick one of the issues that can cause conflict in family life, discuss how it could be resolved and note your group's comments here.

_____

_____

_____

Dealing with conflict

Every family has disagreements from time to time. Arguments are a normal part of family life and can even be healthy. The important thing is to be able to manage these confrontations in the right way. There are many different ways of dealing with conflict. Below are some examples.

● **Count to 10:** This simple exercise gives you a little time to calm down and avoid saying or doing something you may regret later.

● **Walk away:** While not solving the problem, removing yourself from the confrontation will give everyone some space and time to cool off. Go for a walk or meet a friend.

● **Sit down and talk:** Choose a time when everyone has calmed down and try to use some of the assertive communication skills you learned about in First Year. Be honest about your feelings but be open to listening to what the other person has to say. Try to look at different options or solutions and be willing to compromise.

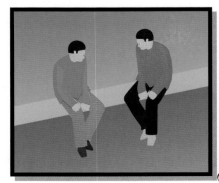

- **Write a letter:** If you find sitting down and talking difficult, try to write a letter explaining how you feel.

- **Talk to someone:** This may give you a fresh way of looking at the conflict and it might even provide new strategies for handling the disagreement.

> You may feel overwhelmed by family conflict sometimes or you might even feel that you are in danger. If this happens, it is important that you find a trusted adult and ask for help.

Changing roles and expectations

As you get older you will have different expectations about how much freedom you should have: you might expect to be allowed out to a disco or to have increased access to social media. Your parents may also give you more responsibilities at home such as looking after younger siblings or helping around the house with different chores. In the Murphy household, we saw that Eoin and Brid's parents expected them to take responsibility to organise their sports gear and make their own lunches. We also saw that Brid expected more freedom around her appearance.

INDIVIDUAL ACTIVITY

Knowing myself

Take a few minutes to reflect on the changes you have experienced in your life around roles and expectations and then answer these questions.

1. Write down some of the tasks and responsibilities you have in your family.

2. Write down how your role has changed in your family as you have grown older.

LEARNING KEEPSAKE

Three things I have learned in this lesson are:

1. _____
2. _____
3. _____

Something that helped me learn in this lesson was:

_____

_____

_____

As a result of this lesson, I will:

_____

_____

_____

_____ has shared this Learning Keepsake with me _____

Name of student   *Parent's/Guardian's signature*

 **LESSON 12**

Stereotyping and Discrimination

Learning outcomes: 1.8, 1.9

responsible · connected · aware · respected

By the end of this lesson you will:

➡ understand stereotyping and its effects

➡ understand how stereotyping can influence the treatment and the rights of people

➡ recognise the contribution you can make to ensure others feel respected and included

KEYWORDS

Stereotyping
Prejudice
Discrimination

 **GROUP ACTIVITY**

Listening and expressing myself

Respecting difference

As a group, write down any words or phrases that immediately come to mind when you think of the following people:

An Irish person	
A biker with lots of tattoos and piercings	
A person from Jamaica	
A group of teenage boys in hoodies hanging around the park	
A pensioner	
A model	
A professional soccer player	
A baby girl	

CLASS DISCUSSION

Discussing/Debating

Stereotyping

We all have images that pop into our head when we think of a particular type of person or group of people. These are stereotypes. Some stereotypes are harmless, e.g. all Italians like pasta. These ideas are fine as long as they don't affect our attitude and behaviour towards other individuals.

> **STEREOTYPING:** Having an over-simplified opinion about a particular group or an individual belonging to a group. If these opinions are negative, they can lead to prejudice and discrimination.
>
> **PREJUDICE (TO 'PREJUDGE'):** Making negative assumptions about a person simply because they belong to a certain social group. For example, 'All young people are rowdy'; 'Old people are boring'.
>
> **DISCRIMINATION:** The unfair treatment of people or groups of people based on the group, category or class to which they are perceived to belong.

INDIVIDUAL ACTIVITY

Reading with understanding

Read the following scenario. Imagine yourself in the situation and answer the questions that follow.

A Day in Town

You and your friends meet in town on a Saturday afternoon. You need to buy a present for your sister's birthday and you head to the bookshop. As you walk around the shop, laughing and joking with each other, you notice the shop security guard is following your group. The sales assistant is also watching you while serving other customers. She approaches your group and says you need

77

to buy something quickly or leave. The shop is busy with groups of adults and families, also browsing, but the sales assistant is not concerned with them. You all leave the shop. Before you get the bus home, one of you wants to buy a bottle of Coke, so you all head to the local corner shop to wait for them while they get it. When you walk in, the shopkeeper immediately asks you to leave as he says he does not want large groups in his store. You notice a family in the store; he doesn't seem to have a problem with them. You get on the bus to go home. You notice people looking at you and your friends and shaking their heads.

1. How do you think you would feel at the end of this day?

_____

_____

_____

2. Why do you think you and your friends were treated unfairly?

_____

_____

_____

3. Have you ever been treated unfairly just because you are young? Explain what happened and how it made you feel.

_____

_____

_____

4. Can you think of other people in our society who are discriminated against because they belong to a certain social group?

_____

_____

_____

5. How do you think this affects their rights and wellbeing?

_____

_____

Why do we stereotype?

We stereotype people for a number of reasons. We may be influenced by the media or our family, friends and peers, or it may be because of a personal experience. Stereotyping is often the result of misinformation or false attitudes and opinions.

The impact of stereotyping

Stereotyping can give rise to discrimination. This can lead to individuals or groups being treated badly or unfairly. Discrimination can deprive people of their rights and reduce their opportunities that many others take for granted, for example in areas of employment and social activities. In Ireland, there are laws in place to protect people from discrimination and harassment. These laws help to promote equality in Irish society.

  INDIVIDUAL ACTIVITY

Reading with understanding

Contributing to making the world a better place

It is against the law to discriminate against a person on the following nine specific grounds. Read them and then write down three reasons why you think they are important laws.

1. GENDER:
You cannot be treated unfairly or differently because you are a man or a woman or transgender.

2. CIVIL STATUS:
You cannot be treated unfairly or differently based on your family situation. This includes being single, married, in a civil union, adopted, separated, divorced, a member of a single-parent family, or widowed.

3. FAMILY STATUS:
You cannot be treated unfairly or differently because you are pregnant, a parent of a person under 18 or a carer of a person with a disability.

4. SEXUAL ORIENTATION:
You cannot be treated unfairly or differently because you are gay, lesbian, bisexual or heterosexual.

5. RELIGION:
You cannot be treated unfairly or differently because of your religious background, religious beliefs, or having no religious background or belief.

6. AGE:
You cannot be treated unfairly or differently because of your age. This ground for discrimination only applies to people over the age of 18, except for the provision of car insurance to licensed drivers under 18.

7. RACE:
You cannot be treated unfairly or differently because you belong to a particular race, or because of your skin colour, nationality or ethnic origin.

8. COMMUNITY:
You cannot be treated unfairly or differently because you are a member of a particular community, e.g. the Travelling community.

9. DISABILITY:
You cannot be treated unfairly or differently if you have a physical, mental or learning disability or a particular medical condition.

These anti-discrimination laws are important because:

Reason 1: _____

_____

Reason 2: _____

_____

Reason 3: _____

_____

What can I do to ensure everyone is treated equally and fairly?

It is important to recognise that everyone has a right to be treated with respect and dignity. We can all do simple things in life to bring about positive changes and stop discrimination. Make a conscious decision to make everyone feel included. By taking leadership against discrimination, we can help break down barriers of prejudice and help prevent discrimination.

INDIVIDUAL ACTIVITY

Making considered decisions

Contributing to making the world a better place

In the hand diagram, write down five things that you can pledge to do as an individual to ensure that all people are respected and included.

I pledge to

LEARNING KEEPSAKE

Three things I have learned in this lesson are:

1. _____
2. _____
3. _____

Something that helped me learn in this lesson was:

_____

_____

_____

As a result of this lesson, I will:

_____

_____

_____

_____ has shared this Learning Keepsake with me _____

Name of student

Parent's/Guardian's signature

MINDING MYSELF & MINDING OTHERS

STRAND 2

TOPIC 1
Being Healthy

Diet, Oh Sugar!

Learning outcome: 2.1

responsible   aware

By the end of this lesson you will:

•→ understand that there are different types of sugars
•→ appreciate the importance of reducing added sugars in your diet
•→ be able to make healthy decisions about your food choices

KEYWORD

Recommendations

USEFUL WEBSITE

www.safefoods.eu Provides tips and information on nutrition and healthy eating.

What is sugar?

When you hear the word 'sugar' and think about how unhealthy it is, you probably think that all sugars are bad, but this is not the case. There are good sugars as well as bad sugars.

Good sugars

These are sugars that occur naturally in foods such as milk, fruit and vegetables. These foods are rich in important nutrients such as fibre, vitamin C and calcium and have various health benefits.

Bad sugars

These sugars are referred to as 'added sugars'. They are added to foods and drinks by manufacturers, chefs and consumers to make them more palatable. Foods that are high in added sugar include fizzy drinks, confectionery, biscuits, cereals and sweetened pastries. However, added sugar can also be found in products we may not consider 'sweet', such as processed foods and sauces like tomato sauce and mayonnaise.

Why do we need to cut down on 'added sugar'?

Many foods and drinks that contain 'added sugar' are high in calories and have few or no other nutrients. Recent evidence has linked a high intake of added sugar to an increased risk of weight gain and chronic illnesses such as heart disease, cancer and type 2 diabetes. It is also linked to dental decay.

How can you tell how much 'added sugar' is in food?

The 'of which sugars' section on a nutrition label provides us with information about the amount of sugar in the product.

For some products like fizzy drinks, confectionery, biscuits, cereals and sweetened pastries, the amount of added sugar is clear from the food label. However, for other products, which also contain natural sugars, it can be difficult to work out how much of the total sugar content is added sugar and how much is natural sugar. Muesli is a good example. The food label on muesli will show a high sugar content, but some of this sugar comes from the dried fruit, which provides good natural sugars.

It is recommended that children from age 11 to adult should have no more than 30 g of 'added sugar' per day. That is the equivalent of seven teaspoons of added sugar per day (4 g of sugar = 1 teaspoon).

A little sugar = 5 g or less per 100 g	A lot of sugar = 15 g or more per 100 g

The ingredients list

All added sugars must be included in the food's ingredients list. Ingredients are listed in descending order of weight, so the higher up the ingredient list that sugar appears, the more sugar the product contains. Be aware that sugar can be sometimes listed under other names including fructose, glucose, sucrose and maltose.

Learning with others   Calculating

PAIR ACTIVITY

In pairs, look at the food labels for the different foods and work out how many teaspoons of sugar are in one serving of that product. Remember 4 g = 1 teaspoon.

Teaspoons of sugar: _____	Teaspoons of sugar: _____	Teaspoons of sugar: _____	Teaspoons of sugar: _____	Teaspoons of sugar: _____

INDIVIDUAL ACTIVITY

Calculating

1. Look at Fred's diet for the day and calculate how much added sugar he uses.

MEAL	GRAMS OF ADDED SUGAR IN EACH ITEM (APPROX.)	TEASPOONS OF SUGAR (4 g = 1 teaspoon, so divide the number of grams by 4)
Breakfast		
50 g bowl of cereal	6 g	
Two slices of bread	4 g	
Chocolate spread	17 g	
200 ml fruit juice	12 g	
Lunch		
½ tin of tomato soup	10 g	
Bagel	6 g	
Yoghurt	9 g	
Dinner		
½ pizza	8 g	
Can of Coke	40 g	
Snack		
Two chocolate biscuits	16 g	
Total daily intake of sugar	_____ grams	_____ teaspoons of sugar

2. What did you notice about the amount of added sugar Fred consumes compared to the amount recommended by health experts?

_____

_____

_____

How to reduce the amount of added sugar in your diet

☛ Replace fizzy or carbonated drinks with milk or water.

☛ Choose fresh foods instead of processed foods.

☛ Use food labels as a guide to choosing foods with less added sugar.

☛ Keep sweetened foods as a treat rather than making them a regular item in your diet.

☛ Reduce the amount of fruit juices listing 'added sugar' that you drink.

☛ If the food contains some added sugar, check that it provides other nutrients too, e.g. fibre or calcium.

LEARNING KEEPSAKE

Three things I have learned in this lesson are:

1. _____

2. _____

3. _____

Something that helped me learn in this lesson was:

_____

_____

_____

As a result of this lesson, I will:

_____

_____

_____

_____ has shared this Learning Keepsake with me _____

Name of student   *Parent's/Guardian's signature*

85

LESSON 14

Physical Activity

Learning outcome: 2.1

responsible   aware

By the end of this lesson you will:

↠ understand the benefits of exercise for your wellbeing
↠ know the types of exercise that are necessary for wellbeing

KEYWORDS

Physical Exercise

!!

Everyone knows that exercise is important for physical wellbeing. However, there are many myths about exercise. The following activity will test how much you know about the 'facts of exercise'.

 INDIVIDUAL ACTIVITY

Thinking critically

1. What do you know about exercise? Tick 'True' or 'False' in relation to each statement.

STATEMENT	TRUE	FALSE
I heard … 'When it comes to exercise, "No Pain No Gain".'	☐	☐
I heard … '60 minutes of straight exercise is better than 10 minutes six times a day.'	☐	☐
I heard … 'Sports drinks are better than water during exercise.'	☐	☐
I heard … 'Wearing heavy clothes during exercise will make me sweat more, so I'll lose weight faster.'	☐	☐
I heard … 'Drinking water before and during physical activity will give me a stitch in my side.'	☐	☐
I heard … 'If I stop being active, the muscles I have built will turn to fat.'	☐	☐
I heard … 'Physical activity that zaps my energy will leave me too tired to do anything afterwards.'	☐	☐
I heard … 'Physical activity is only worthwhile if I'm really good at it, or if I do it for a long time.'	☐	☐

STATEMENT	TRUE	FALSE
I heard … 'People with asthma can partake in physical activity.'	☐	☐
I heard … 'Exercising outside when it's really hot can be risky.'	☐	☐
I heard … 'Some types of physical activity are better for my bones than others.'	☐	☐
I heard … 'It doesn't matter what you eat if you are exercising.'	☐	☐
I heard … 'Exercising too much can cause burnout.'	☐	☐

2. When you have established with your teacher which of these are true and which are false, were there any that surprised you?

_____

_____

The Physical Activity Pyramid

The Physical Activity Pyramid shows different ways to stay active and how often you need to exercise to stay fit and healthy. In the blank boxes you see in the pyramid below, write down the number of times you participate in each of the levels of activity. Then answer the questions on the next page.

The Physical Activity Pyramid

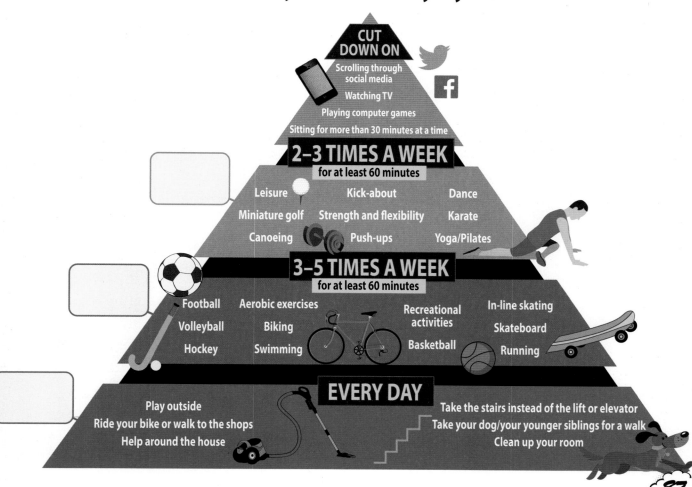

INDIVIDUAL ACTIVITY

Knowing
myself

Being healthy
and physically active

1. What does the pyramid tell you about your current levels of physical activity?

_____

_____

2. What changes, if any, could you make to your pyramid to improve your level of physical activity?

_____

_____

If you are inactive:

● Start off slowly, doing activities from the bottom of the pyramid on one to two days a week.

● When you feel comfortable with this, aim for 30 minutes of activity most days in the week; for example, increase from 30 minutes on 2 to 3 days a week to 30 minutes on 3 to 4 days a week.

● Become more active for longer; be active for 60 minutes or more on some days and choose a more vigorous activity.

● As you progress, you will get closer to the goal of 60 minutes or more of moderate to vigorous physical activity every day.

(Source: The National Guidelines on Physical Activity for Ireland)

Listening and
expressing myself

In groups, read the messages on the screens. Give three reasons for each screen statement.

4 out of 5 children
do not get the
recommended 60
minutes of physical
activity per day.

Reason 1: _____

Reason 2: _____

Reason 3: _____

In 1975, one in every
100 Irish children
were obese. Now
it's 1 in every 10.

Reason 1: _____

Reason 2: _____

Reason 3: _____

89

Benefits of physical activity

Stimulates growth of brain cells

Improves mood

Improves sleep

Reduces stress

Reduces tension

Improves appetite

Keeps you motivated

Improves digestion

Increases attention

Improves learning

Releases endorphins

Helps to burn fat

Improves self-image

Reduces anxiety

Strengthens muscles

Boosts productivity

Increases agility

Makes you feel better

Improves happiness

Boosts creativity

Improves blood flow

Reduces cholesterol

Prevents muscle loss

Improves cognitive functioning

Lowers risk of cancer

Improves performance at school

Prevents colds

Strengthens your heart

Strengthens bones

Increases speed

Makes you smile

Improves sports endurance

Improves immune system

Improves motor skills

Controls your weight

Improves balance

Improves awareness

Improves fitness

Improves performance

Improves breathing

Reduces fatigue

Increases focus

Increases stamina

Boosts energy

Improves flexibility

Increases strength

Decreases body fat

Improves body image

Increases confidence

Lowers resting heart rate

Knowing
myself

Being healthy and
physically active

INDIVIDUAL ACTIVITY

Fill in your own Physical Activity Pyramid. Write in the activities you currently do and any additional activities you could do in the first three levels, and add the activities you could cut down on in the fourth level.

The Physical Activity Pyramid

CUT
DOWN ON

2–3 TIMES A WEEK

3–5 TIMES A WEEK

EVERY DAY

LEARNING KEEPSAKE

Three things I have learned in this lesson are:

1. _____
2. _____
3. _____

As a result of what I have learned about physical activity, I will:

_____

_____

_____

As a result of this lesson, I will:

_____

_____

_____

_____ has shared this Learning Keepsake with me _____

Name of student   *Parent's/Guardian's signature*

LESSON 15 Sleep

Learning outcome: 2.1

By the end of this lesson you will:

→ recognise the contribution of sleep to your overall health and wellbeing

→ analyse your own sleep patterns and make necessary changes

KEYWORD

Sleep deprivation

Sleep is very important for our overall health and wellbeing. According to the Mental Health Foundation, we cannot function effectively without sleep. Teenagers and babies need a lot of sleep as their bodies are still growing. Studies have shown, however, that many teenagers are not getting enough sleep.

Being healthy

INDIVIDUAL ACTIVITY

Read the statements and decide whether you think they are 'True' or 'False'.

STATEMENT	TRUE	FALSE
A teenager needs more sleep than a newborn baby.	☐	☐
You should avoid eating too much before going to bed.	☐	☐
It is a good idea to sleep in at the weekends as it energises you for the week ahead.	☐	☐
Teenagers' social media use is reducing the amount they sleep.	☐	☐
It is a good idea to relax before bed with a cup of tea.	☐	☐
Sleep deprivation is implicated in one in five road deaths in Ireland.	☐	☐
Drinking alcohol helps you sleep better.	☐	☐
Poor sleeping habits can cause weight gain.	☐	☐
It should take 10–15 minutes to fall asleep each night.	☐	☐
It is harder for teenagers to fall asleep.	☐	☐

A good night's sleep is important because ...

- It re-energises and repairs our body. Just as a mobile phone needs to be charged regularly, we need to recharge our body so we will be ready for the following day.

- It helps to protect us against disease and illness.

- It helps us to cope better with life's challenges – lack of sleep is associated with poor mental health.

- It allows our brains to recharge, improving concentration in school.

- It can help us perform better at physical activities.

AGE GROUP	RECOMMENDED NUMBER OF HOURS OF SLEEP
Newborns (0–3 months)	14–17 hours
Infants (4–11 months)	12–15 hours
Toddlers (1–2 years)	11–14 hours
Preschoolers (3–5)	10–13 hours
School-age children (6–13)	9–11 hours
Teenagers (14–17)	8–10 hours
Young adults (18–25)	7–9 hours
Adults (26–64)	7–9 hours
Seniors (65 and older)	7–8 hours

Some interesting facts about sleep

- Regular exercise helps you sleep more soundly.

- Humans spend one-third of their lives sleeping.

- Two-thirds of a cat's life is spent sleeping.

- A giraffe only needs 1.9 hours of sleep a day.

- Within five minutes of waking, up to 50 per cent of our dreams are forgotten.

- The record for the longest time without sleep is 11 days.

- Dysania is the name for finding it hard to get out of bed in the morning.

- Humans are the only mammals who delay sleep.

- Napping during the day is not a good idea as it makes sleeping at night more difficult.

- Over the last century we have been getting less sleep.

- The blue light emitted by electronic devices inhibits the production of melatonin, the hormone that controls your sleep. A reduced amount of melatonin makes it harder to fall asleep and stay asleep.

The stages of sleep

There are five stages of sleep. Each of these stages serves a different purpose. You will go through all five stages several times (on average four to six times) each night, but not always in the same order.

Stage 1: This is a short stage where you feel yourself drifting off. You could be easily woken at this stage.

Stage 2: Brain activity, heart rate and breathing slow down. You begin to reach a state of relaxation.

Stage 3: Deep sleep. Your body repairs tissue and builds bone. If you were woken at this stage, you would be very drowsy and confused.

Stage 4: The deepest stage of sleep.

Stage 5: Dream stage, also known as REM (rapid eye movement) sleep. The activity of your brainwaves is similar to when you are awake.

Tips for a good night's sleep

- Stick to the same routine – get up and go to bed at a similar time each morning and night.
- Don't go to bed too hungry or too full.
- Avoid drinks that contain caffeine, such as tea, coffee or Coke, for four hours before going to bed.
- Create a room that is comfortable for sleeping in – it should be cool, dark and quiet.
- Leave all electronic gadgets in another room.
- Do something calming before going to bed such as taking a bath, reading a book, listening to music, or doing breathing exercises.
- Placing lavender drops on your pillow can help you relax and so fall asleep quicker.
- Cut down on daytime naps; if you do take a nap, limit it to twenty minutes.
- Try to sort out your worries before you go to bed, e.g. if something is troubling you, write it down on a piece of paper and set it aside to deal with the next day.
- If you are still finding it difficult to fall asleep, concentrate on your breathing – count each in-breath and out-breath.

INDIVIDUAL ACTIVITY

Being healthy

For the next week, monitor your sleeping habits.

NIGHT	TIME I WENT TO BED	TIME I GOT UP	HOURS SLEPT	BEFORE I WENT TO BED I ...
Monday				
Tuesday				
Wednesday				
Thursday				
Friday				
Saturday				
Sunday				

1. What does the chart tell you about your sleep habits?

_____

_____

_____

2. How might you need to adapt your habits to ensure that you are getting enough sleep?

_____

_____

_____

LEARNING KEEPSAKE

Three things I have learned in this lesson are:

1. _____

2. _____

3. _____

Something that helped me learn in this lesson was:

_____

_____

_____

As a result of this lesson, I will:

_____

_____

_____

_____ has shared this Learning Keepsake with me _____

Name of student   *Parent's/Guardian's signature*

LESSON 16

Sense of Belonging

Learning outcome: 2.3

 responsible

 connected

resilient

 aware

By the end of this lesson you will:

- appreciate the importance of making connections and how to create a sense of belonging
- be able to describe what promotes a sense of belonging in school, at home and in the wider community
- recognise your own role in creating an inclusive environment

KEYWORD

Belonging

USEFUL WEBSITE

www.spunout.ie Youth information website created by young people for young people providing information and articles on a wide range of topics affecting young people.

 GROUP ACTIVITY

Knowing myself

In First Year, you learned about what it means to be healthy and to have a balanced life. In groups, discuss and then write down three things for each element that you can do to ensure that your life is balanced.

EMOTIONAL (MENTAL)

SOCIAL

HEALTH

PHYSICAL

PHYSICAL
1.
2.
3.

SOCIAL
1.
2.
3.

EMOTIONAL (MENTAL)
1.
2.
3.

97

A sense of belonging

A big part of our social health is about making connections. A sense of belonging is the feeling of being connected and accepted within our family and community. It is one of our most basic human needs, just like food and shelter. We all have different needs, with some people enjoying more connections with other people and some enjoying less. The desire to belong lasts our whole life, yet our sense of belonging can be easily damaged by just one instance of isolation or exclusion from a group.

Knowing myself

Write the initials of your group's members in the centre of the diagram. In the next circle, write some family activities that help to give each member a sense of belonging, e.g. sitting together to eat, doing chores, family outings and functions, looking after younger brothers or sisters, movie nights. In the next circle, write things that happen in your school to make people feel that they belong, e.g. school trips, sports teams, shows, pastoral care groups. In the outer circle, write the things that happen in your community that instil a sense of belonging, e.g. Tidy Towns volunteering, coaching a team, becoming a member of the Red Cross, local park runs, volunteering.

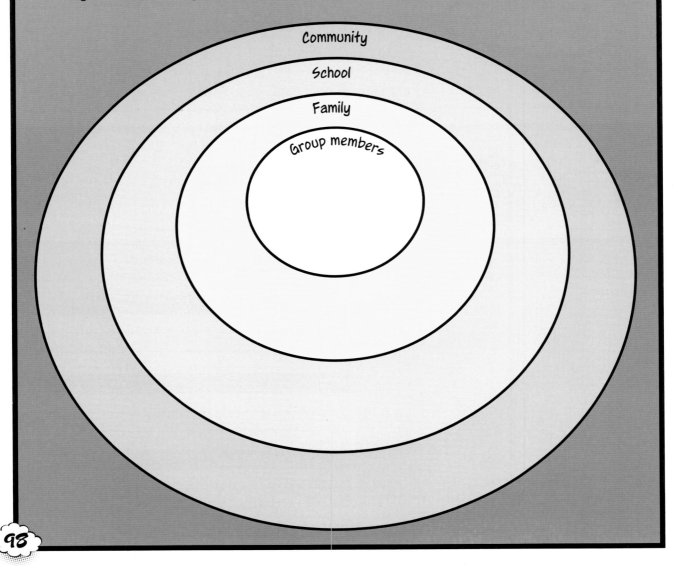

Why is a sense of belonging so important?

Throughout history, belonging to a tribe has helped people to protect and define themselves.

Belonging helps us feel:

- valued, needed and accepted by others
- that our beliefs and opinions are valued
- that we have people who will support us in difficult times

Without a strong sense of belonging we can feel:

- anxious
- isolated
- lonely
- unsupported

There are lots of groups we can belong to, including:

- family
- school
- friends
- sporting groups
- community
- spiritual groups
- online groups
- drama groups

 INDIVIDUAL ACTIVITY

Knowing myself

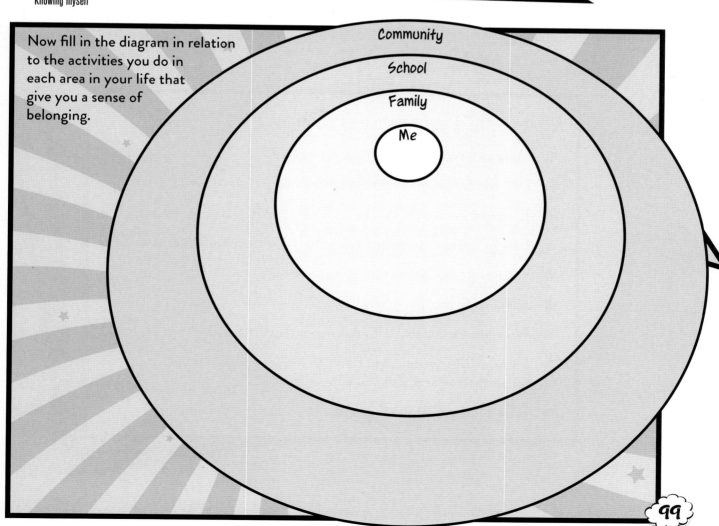

Now fill in the diagram in relation to the activities you do in each area in your life that give you a sense of belonging.

Community

School

Family

Me

What if a person feels they don't belong?

It is very important to us to feel that we belong and that we have made some connections. Of course, from time to time, we can lose connections in our life. This is natural and can happen for a number of reasons:

- Maybe I haven't found my 'tribe' yet.

- Maybe I haven't opened up enough to people, letting them know who I really am.

- Maybe I worry too much about what other people think of me and so don't act like my genuine self.

- Maybe I haven't started 'owning' my uniqueness yet.

- Maybe I'm shy.

- Maybe I try too hard to make others like me.

- Maybe I don't try hard enough or maybe I don't listen.

It is very important that you accept who you are, and know that you will find people who like you for who you are. These are the people who are really worth knowing. Know too that everybody has to make an effort with their friends and everybody likes to feel listened to, valued and respected.

How to build your sense of belonging

- Make an effort to join in group activities.

- Look out for people who have similar interests to you.

- Try to get involved in a club that focuses on one of your interests.

- Take an interest in other people's lives; don't just talk about yourself.

- Volunteer for a cause you are interested in.

- Join a social group.

- Write letters to people; it's fun when they write back.

- Focus on what you have in common with the people around you, rather then what makes you different.

- Have a 'say yes' motto if people invite you to do something.

 At other times, feeling disconnected and as if you don't belong might be caused by more serious issues such as mental illness or bereavement. If you are feeling cut off or isolated for these reasons, it is important that you talk with a trusted friend, adult or a health professional.

LEARNING KEEPSAKE

Three things I have learned in this lesson are:

1. _____

2. _____

3. _____

Something that helped me learn in this lesson was:

_____

_____

_____

As a result of this lesson, I will:

_____

_____

_____

_____ has shared this Learning Keepsake with me _____

Name of student   *Parent's/Guardian's signature*

MEET THE CHALLENGE

Strand 2 Topic 1
'KNOW YOUR ADDED SUGARS' AWARENESS CAMPAIGN

Learning outcomes: 1.7, 2.1

Your class wishes to raise awareness on the added sugar content of some foods and drinks commonly consumed by young people. As a class:

○ brainstorm a list of high-sugar food and drinks that are popular among young people

○ pick ten of these high-sugar products enjoyed by young people

○ using 'teaspoons of sugar' as the measurement, research the sugar content of each of these ten products

Then, working in two groups, select five products each and design a chart showing the added sugar content of those products. The chart should include:

○ a picture of the product

○ how many teaspoons of sugar it contains

○ how much sugar would be consumed by a person if they ate this product once a day for one year

○ the effects that too much sugar can have on our physical health

○ the effects that too much sugar can have on our mental wellbeing

TOPIC 2
Anti-Bullying

School Anti-Bullying Policy

Learning outcome: 2.12

 responsible

 connected

 resilient

 respected

 aware

By the end of this lesson you will:

⇥ be more familiar with your school's anti-bullying policy

⇥ be more aware of your school's 'Acceptable Internet Usage Policy'

⇥ have revised the consequences for students who take part in bullying behaviour

⇥ have identified ways to make your school a bully-free zone

KEYWORDS

Anti-bullying policy

Acceptable usage policy

Internet safety

USEFUL WEBSITES

www.barnardos.ie Provides information and advice on how to deal with bullying.

www.childnet.com Provides blogs and advice for young people on how to use the internet safely, responsibly and positively.

School should be a safe environment for every child and adult. One way to help ensure this is to prevent bullying. All schools are obliged to adopt and follow an anti-bullying policy. It is important for you to be familiar with your school's anti-bullying and ICT acceptable use policies (AUP) as many of the school's general rules are contained in these policies.

INDIVIDUAL ACTIVITY

Being safe

Reflect on your knowledge of or opinions on your school's anti-bullying and ICT acceptable use policies by ticking 'Yes' or 'No' for the following statements.

STATEMENT	YES	NO
I am aware of the different types of bullying.	☐	☐
I am protected by my school from bullying.	☐	☐
My school is supportive of people who are bullied.	☐	☐
I believe that students have a role to play in the prevention of bullying.	☐	☐
I believe that parents have a role to play in the prevention of bullying.	☐	☐
I believe teachers have a role to play in the prevention of bullying.	☐	☐
Our school is a safe place to be LGBTQ+.	☐	☐
Our school is a safe place for all students.	☐	☐
I know my role in respecting and protecting someone who is being bullied.	☐	☐
I know where to find the ICT acceptable use policy for my school.	☐	☐

GROUP ACTIVITY

Being safe   Learning with others

In groups, read the following Anti-Bullying Policy sample and ICT Acceptable Use Policy sample. Then read the scenarios that follow and, in each case, decide if the terms of either policy were breached.

If possible, use your school's policies in deciding if their terms were breached in the scenarios given. If they are not available, use the samples provided.

SAMPLE: ANTI-BULLYING POLICY

This policy aims to create a safe learning environment that:

➡ is welcoming of difference and diversity

➡ is based on inclusivity

➡ encourages students to disclose and discuss incidents of bullying behaviour in a non-threatening environment

➡ promotes respectful relationships across the school community

➡ explicitly address the issues of cyberbullying and identity-based bullying including homophobic and transphobic bullying

Definition of bullying

Bullying is unwanted negative behaviour – verbal, psychological or physical – conducted by an individual or group against another person or persons, and which is repeated over time.

The following types of bullying behaviour are included in the definition of bullying:

➡ Deliberate exclusion, malicious gossip and other forms of relational bullying

➡ Physical aggression

➡ Damage to property

➡ Name-calling

➡ Slagging

➡ Offensive graffiti

➡ Insulting, offensive gestures

➡ Intimidation

➡ Relational bulling – taking someone's friends away, exclusion, ignoring and or mocking someone

➡ Cyberbullying – posting offensive or aggressive messages under another person's name; continually sending vicious, mean or disturbing messages to someone; spreading rumours, lies or gossip to hurt a person's reputation

➡ Identity-based bullying such as homophobic and racist bullying, bullying of those with disabilities or special educational needs

➡ Sexual bullying/harassment – unwelcome or inappropriate sexual comments or touching/harassment

Isolated or once-off incidents of intentional negative behaviour, including a once-off offensive or hurtful message, do not fall within the definition of bullying and will be dealt with, as appropriate, in accordance with the school's code of behaviour. However, a once-off offensive or hurtful public message, image or statement on a social network site or other public place where the message can be viewed and/or repeated by other people is regarded as bullying behaviour.

Reporting bullying

If you wish to report an incident of bullying, please talk to any of the following relevant teachers:

➡ Principal

➡ Deputy principal

➡ Year head

Any teacher may act as a relevant teacher if circumstances warrant it.

All teaching and non-teaching staff such as secretaries, caretakers, etc. must report any incidents of bullying behaviour witnessed by them or mentioned to them to the relevant teacher.

Parents are asked to co-operate fully with any investigations into bullying.

Sanctions

As bullying behaviour is against school rules, a student who persists in bullying behaviour will be subject to the appropriate sanctions:

1. Lunchtime detention

2. After-school detention

3. School community tasks – picking up litter or light cleaning duties out of school hours

4. Exclusion from school-organised events and activities.

SAMPLE: ICT ACCEPTABLE USE POLICY

In accordance with the ICT Acceptable Use Policy, students must:

1. Not damage ICT equipment or any part of the school's ICT facilities
2. Not install software from the internet or bring software into school
3. Not share passwords with others or use other people's passwords
4. Not interfere with or delete other students' files
5. Not interfere with or delete the files of any members of staff
6. Report any accidental accessing of inappropriate materials
7. Ask permission before using the internet
8. Not access online gaming sites or any other information that is not relevant to their studies
9. Not copy material from the internet and pass it off as their own
10. Ensure that any work they publish on the internet will not be offensive
11. Accept that their internet usage may be monitored for security and management reasons

12. Not send or receive material that is inappropriate, offensive or illegal
13. Never arrange a face-to-face meeting with someone they know only through emails or the internet
14. Only access chat rooms, discussion forums, messaging or other electronic communications that have been approved by the school. These forums will only be used for educational purposes.
15. Not use their mobile phone during school hours. Mobile phones must be turned off and placed in lockers during school hours.

For each of the fictional scenarios below and on the next page, discuss these three questions and then write your answers into the spaces provided:

1. Does this incident breach the terms of the school's anti-bullying policy and/or ICT AUP? Explain your answer.
2. Who is responsible for resolving this issue? Explain your answer.
3. Should anyone receive a school sanction because of this incident? If so, what should it be and why?

---

1. Jane is talking to her friend Susan on WhatsApp about how annoying and big-headed Joan is since she became captain of the school team. She accidently sends the message to Joan.

Breach?

Who is responsible?

Issue school sanction?/ What should it be and why?

---

2. The boys in geography class have taken a dislike to their teacher, Mr Burke. They decide to put a nasty comment online about him.

Breach?

Who is responsible?

Issue school sanction?/ What should it be and why?

3. Pauline is a very alternative dresser. She doesn't mind if others approve of her fashion or not. She feels very hurt, however, when she sees a number of posters with her name on them and some funny cartoon characters posted around the school.

Breach?

Who is responsible?

Issue school sanction?/ What should it be and why?

4. Callum likes to be organised and prepared for every subject. Sometimes Steven steals and hides Callum's PE gear for a laugh.

Breach?

Who is responsible?

Issue school sanction?/ What should it be and why?

5. Grace and Pippa are in the same group of friends. Whenever the gang are together, Grace makes fun of Pippa: she mocks her accent, makes snide comments about Pippa's appearance and often makes faces and rolls her eyes when Pippa is talking. This makes Pippa very confused because when it is just the two of them, Grace is like her best friend.

Breach?

Who is responsible?

Issue school sanction?/ What should it be and why?

6. Peter is a quiet student. David has never been friendly towards Peter. Recently, after a rugby match where Peter missed a tackle, David called him gay. Later, in the changing rooms, David wrote on the toilet doors, 'Peter is gay'.

Breach?

Who is responsible?

Issue school sanction?/ What should it be and why?

7. The basketball team are in high spirits after winning their match. For a laugh, Eric takes a picture of Paul in the shower and shares it with rest of the team. It is not long before it has gone around the whole school. Paul is only alerted to it when his sister gets the message.

Breach?

Who is responsible?

Issue school sanction?/ What should it be and why?

Being safe

Learning with others

CLASS ACTIVITY

Imagine a school without bullying. We are now going to create a charter that promotes a bully-free environment in your school. A charter is a contract of agreement among a group of people. Consider your school's anti-bullying policy and ICT acceptable usage policy and come to an agreement on what behaviours are necessary to promote a bully-free school. Try to use positive rather than negative statements, e.g. 'Look out for others'; 'Say hi to someone new at break-time'; 'Walk in someone else's shoes'.

OUR CLASS'S ANTI-BULLYING CHARTER

LEARNING KEEPSAKE

Three things I have learned in this lesson are:

1. _____
2. _____
3. _____

Something that helped me learn in this lesson was:

_____

_____

_____

As a result of this lesson, I will:

_____

_____

_____

_____ has shared this Learning Keepsake with me _____

Name of student   *Parent's/Guardian's signature*

LESSON 18
Cyberbullying

Learning outcomes: 2.10, 2.11

responsible · connected · resilient · respected · aware

By the end of this lesson you will:

↠ be able to identify the different types of cyberbullying

↠ know the necessary steps to take if you are being cyberbullied

↠ realise the effects of cyberbullying on a person's wellbeing

KEYWORD

Cyberbullying

USEFUL WEBSITES

www.spunout.ie Youth information website created by young people for young people. Includes articles on cyberbullying.

www.kidshealth.org Provides information on how to deal with cyberbullying.

!!

Information technologies have changed how people communicate. Despite the many benefits of mobile phones and social media, they also open up opportunities for misuse such as in instances of cyberbullying.

CYBERBULLYING is the use of electronic communication to harass or intimidate a person. It is behaviour that is repeated, aggressive and intentional.

Being social; Using language
being safe

INDIVIDUAL ACTIVITY

Below are definitions of different types of cyberbullying. Read the definitions and then, from the options given in the box, write the type of cyberbullying behaviour described next to its definition.

| Flaming | Catfishing | Denigration | Impersonation |
| Outing | Trickery | Exclusion | Cyberstalking |

CYBERBULLYING BEHAVIOUR	DEFINITION
	Repeatedly sending vicious, hurtful, mean and insulting digital messages to another person
	Creating a fake online profile and sending or posting offensive or aggressive messages with the intention of getting the other person in trouble, damaging their reputation or friendships
	Sharing another person's private information or images online
	Spreading damaging rumours, lies or gossip about someone online to damage their reputation
	The process of befriending or chatting with someone online, while using a fake identity
	Fooling someone into revealing secrets or embarrassing information and sharing it online
	Using vulgar language and insults to provoke an online fight
	Purposely excluding someone from an online group

Advice for dealing with cyberbullying

If you are cyberbullied:

- Remember it is not your fault.

- It may be difficult, but try not to take things personally.

- Do not engage the bully – do not reply to any hurtful messages you receive.

- Save the bullying messages as evidence by taking a screenshot.

- Keep a diary of the bullying behaviour – save any messages and record the dates. This can be used as evidence.

- Make sure the privacy settings on your social networking accounts are such that they prevent others gaining access to your profile.

- Report online abuse to the site administrator. Block the person/people who are bullying you to prevent any further upsetting interactions.

- Change your password if you think someone may have gained access to your account. Think of your password like your toothbrush. Pick a good one, change it regularly and never share it.

- If the bullying persists, it's very important to look for help. Confide in a trusted adult.

If you witness cyberbullying:

- Tell a trusted adult.

- Support the person and let them know they are not alone.

- Make it clear that these messages are not OK.

- Demonstrate respectful online behaviour by writing positive comments.

- Post something nice about the person.

- Talk in private to the person doing the bullying.

If you think you may have posted something online that causes offence:

- Remove the post.

- Apologise to the person and explain that you won't do it again.

- Speak to an adult about what you have done.

Being social; Being safe   Learning with others

1. Below are some scenarios that demonstrate different cyberbullying behaviours. Read each scenario and answer the questions that follow.

Scenario 1

Jane and her friends were hanging out at her house. When Jane went to the kitchen to make tea, she left her Facebook page open and her friends decided to send a spiteful message to Jane's cousin, Clara, who is also in their class. The next day, Clara approached Jane about it.

1. What type of cyberbullying behaviour is this? _____
_____

2. How do you think this behaviour is affecting Jane? _____
_____

3. What would you advise Jane to do in this situation? _____
_____

Scenario 2

When Rachel broke up with Ivan, he sent her many threatening and hurtful messages. He spread nasty stories about her and he posted an inappropriate photo of her online. He makes a nasty comment about every picture or post she puts on Facebook. Sometimes he messages her late at night.

1. What type of cyberbullying behaviour is this? _____
_____

2. How do you think this behaviour is affecting Rachel?_____
_____

3. What would you advise Rachel to do in this situation?_____
_____

Scenario 3

Brian is upset in school one day. After school, one of his classmates, John, sends a message pretending to be his friend and asks him personal questions about why he was upset. Trusting John, Brian reveals that he has feelings for Alex, who is also in their class. John forwards the messages to the class's WhatsApp group, which Alex is also a member of.

1. What type of cyberbullying behaviour is this? _____
_____

2. How do you think this behaviour is affecting Brian? _____
_____

3. What would you advise Brian to do in this situation? _____
_____

113

Scenario 4

Emma has a large group of friends. Belinda appears to be the leader of the group. Emma has sent friend requests on Facebook to a number of girls from the group but they have ignored them. Emma thinks this is because Belinda doesn't like her.

1. What type of cyberbullying behaviour is this? _____

_____

2. How do you think this behaviour is affecting Emma? _____

_____

3. What would you advise Emma to do in this situation? _____

_____

INDIVIDUAL ACTIVITY

Being responsible, safe and ethical in using digital technology

From what you learned in class, what should you do in the following situations?

1. *You are being cyberbullied*
Every time you post a picture on your social media page, a certain group from your school posts nasty and hurtful comments about you.

_____

_____

2. *You witness cyberbullying*
Your friend showed you a fake social media profile of one of your classmates. People have left rude and hurtful comments on this page. He is unaware that this page exists.

_____

_____

3. *You have cyberbullied someone*
You shared an embarrassing picture of a classmate online, and it was reshared many times by other students in your school. He is really upset and you regret doing it now.

_____

_____

LEARNING KEEPSAKE

Three things I have learned in this lesson are:

1. _____

2. _____

3. _____

Something that helped me learn in this lesson was:

_____

_____

_____

As a result of this lesson, I will:

_____

_____

_____

_____

_____ has shared this Learning Keepsake with me _____

Name of student   *Parent's/Guardian's signature*

MEET THE CHALLENGE
Strand 2 Topic 2
'STAND UP TO BULLYING' TALK

Learning outcomes: 2.10, 2.11, 2.12

Write and deliver a talk to First- and Second-Year students to raise awareness of bullying. In your talk:

- ○ introduce yourself and give your reasons for speaking
- ○ give a definition of bullying and name the different types of bullying
- ○ use some anecdotes, facts and statistics to support your points
- ○ point out the school rules that protect students from bullying
- ○ explain the role of bystanders in incidents of bullying
- ○ emphasise who can help
- ○ finish off your speech with strong encouragement to your listeners to stand up to bullying
- ○ thank your audience for listening

TOPIC 3
Respectful Communication

Assertive Communication

Learning outcomes: 2.5, 2.8, 2.9

responsible   connected   resilient   respected   aware

By the end of this lesson you will:

➜ have practised assertive communication skills
➜ be aware of the appropriate uses of assertive communication

KEYWORDS

Communication
Passive
Aggressive
Assertive

USEFUL WEBSITES

www.kidshealth.org Provides information on assertiveness for teens.

www.reachout.com Provides useful information on communication styles.

In First Year, you learned about the difference between assertive, aggressive and passive behaviour. Look at the table on the next page to remind yourself of what each of these terms means.

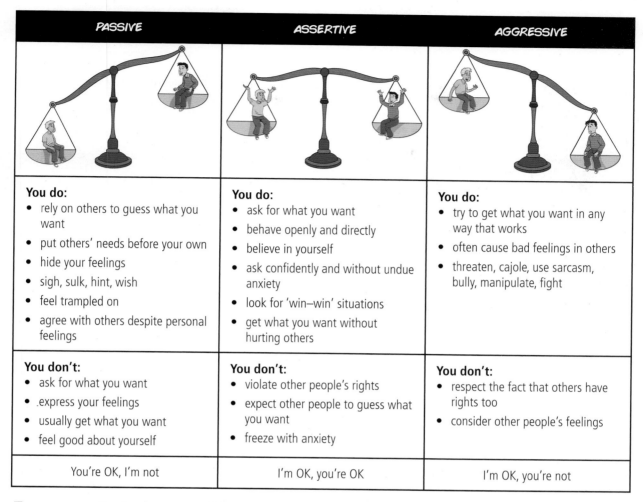

PASSIVE	ASSERTIVE	AGGRESSIVE
You do: • rely on others to guess what you want • put others' needs before your own • hide your feelings • sigh, sulk, hint, wish • feel trampled on • agree with others despite personal feelings	**You do:** • ask for what you want • behave openly and directly • believe in yourself • ask confidently and without undue anxiety • look for 'win–win' situations • get what you want without hurting others	**You do:** • try to get what you want in any way that works • often cause bad feelings in others • threaten, cajole, use sarcasm, bully, manipulate, fight
You don't: • ask for what you want • express your feelings • usually get what you want • feel good about yourself	**You don't:** • violate other people's rights • expect other people to guess what you want • freeze with anxiety	**You don't:** • respect the fact that others have rights too • consider other people's feelings
You're OK, I'm not	I'm OK, you're OK	I'm OK, you're not

Appropriate assertive communication

Although assertive communication skills are very important, there are times when it is not appropriate to use them. If a person is unwell, has received some bad news or is going through a rough patch, you may need to be sensitive to what they are feeling. At other times, an assertive response could be putting your safety at risk, so you need to assess the situation.

GROUP ACTIVITY

Developing good relationships and dealing with conflict

Knowing myself

In groups, think of different situations where assertive communication may not be suitable or appropriate.

Situation 1: _____

Situation 2: _____

Situation 3: _____

Situation 4: _____

INDIVIDUAL ACTIVITY

1. Read the following scenarios and identify each response as passive, aggressive or assertive. The first one has been done for you.

		Assertive	Aggressive	Passive
1.	You have forgotten to do your homework. You: (a) Tell the teacher before class starts (b) Bide your time and hope the teacher won't ask (c) Make up an excuse	a	b	c
2.	A classmate who you thought was your friend keeps making hurtful comments to you in front of others in the class. You: (a) Avoid them in the hope it will go away (b) Challenge them to a fight (c) Approach them and calmly ask them for an explanation			
3.	You are meeting a friend to go to the cinema. She is extremely late, as usual. When she arrives she explains that there was a family emergency: You: (a) Shout at her, 'I've been waiting 20 minutes!' (b) Tell her you understand but you would appreciate it if in future she could text you to say she'll be late (c) Say 'It's ok, I don't mind waiting', even though you do mind			
4.	Your friend has asked to borrow your top again. She borrowed a top three weeks ago and she still hasn't given it back. You say: (a) 'You've got some cheek – you borrowed a top off me three weeks ago and I still haven't seen it. You have no respect for my things.' (b) 'Well, OK, I suppose it is alright.' (c) 'I'm very happy to let you borrow my clothes, but I would appreciate it if you gave them back sooner. I hate having to ask.'			
5.	Your friend asks you to mitch school. You: (a) Go with them even though you don't want to (b) Tell them you have no interest in mitching school (c) Start shouting at them, telling them that they are an idiot to mitch			

6.	Your parents have given you permission to stay out until 9 p.m. It's 10 p.m. by the time you arrive home but you have a good reason for it. When you arrive home, your parents are extremely angry. You: (a) Ignore them and go straight to your room (b) Start shouting back at them (c) Apologise and explain calmly why you are late			
7.	Someone you don't fancy approaches you at the disco and asks you out. You: (a) Laugh at them and say you wouldn't go near them with a barge pole (b) Let them down gently (c) Say yes because you don't want to hurt their feelings			
8.	Your brother borrowed your calculator again without asking. Now you have no calculator for maths class. You: (a) Say nothing and just borrow your friend's calculator (b) Yell at him in front of his friends when you see him at lunch time (c) Wait for a good time to explain calmly that you are upset about it			
9.	Somebody insults you. You: (a) Get very angry and shout back at them (b) Ask them why they said it and tell them how it makes you feel (c) Start to think it is true and get upset because why else would someone say that about you			
10.	Some people in your class who you thought were your friends have organised a day out together but they haven't asked you. You: (a) Speak to one person you are particularly friendly with and ask her why you were not invited (b) Send an angry text to all of them (c) Carry on as normal and pretend you are not upset			
11.	You are having a meal in a restaurant and the waiter brings you lukewarm soup. You (a) Eat it and say nothing (b) Call the waiter over and tell him politely that the soup is not hot enough (c) Click your fingers when you see the waiter nearby to call him over, and then complain loudly			

12.	You fancy someone in your year. You: (a) Approach them to see if they would like to do something sometime (b) Make your friend tell them that you like them and ask them to get an answer as to whether they like you too (c) Say nothing and hope they get the hint			
13.	One of your friends wants to copy your homework. You say: (a) 'I suppose so, just make sure to drop it back to me before class.' (b) 'I don't like people copying my homework, sorry.' (c) 'Get lost. Do your own homework!'			

2. Now that you are aware of which responses are passive, aggressive or assertive, circle the responses you would be most likely to make in these situations and record your results below.

Number of passive responses I would make	
Number of assertive responses I would make	
Number of aggressive responses I would make	

GROUP ACTIVITY

Developing good relationships and dealing with conflict

Knowing myself

In small groups, role-play an assertive response to one of the situations on the cards below. Your teacher will assign one to your group.

You are meeting your friend in town. She is late as usual. You are getting tired of this.

You are hanging out with a group of friends in the park. Another friend joins you with a crate of beers. Your friends take a bottle and offer one to you.

You bought a new jacket. After returning home, you notice that there is a rip under the arm. When you return it to the store, the shop assistant claims that the rip is your fault.

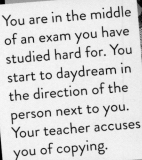

You are in the middle of an exam you have studied hard for. You start to daydream in the direction of the person next to you. Your teacher accuses you of copying.

You and your friends are doing a science project together. One person is dictating the way the group should be organised and which tasks each person should get. You are not happy with your task as you feel it's the most difficult one.

Your teacher finds your name written on a desk. He accuses you of doing it.

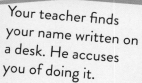

You are wearing your new jacket to the disco. When you meet your friend, she says it doesn't suit you.

You changed your plans to help a friend with an essay. She never turned up. You meet her before class.

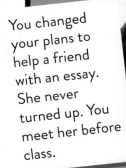

Tips for assertive communication

Stand or sit up straight.

Make eye contact but don't glare at the other person.

Keep your voice calm – do not whine and do not shout.

Look firm but be aware of looking aggressive.

Use clear, direct statements, e.g. 'Would you please return my top?' rather than 'Would you mind returning my top?'

Say what you have to say and stick to it.

When refusing a request, say 'no' clearly. If you are unsure, do not make a rushed decision – say you will think about it and get back to the other person.

Never make it personal. Use 'I' statements, e.g. 'I feel when …' rather than'You' statements, e.g. 'You always do this ...'

If you are meeting someone to discuss something you are not happy about, pick a good time when you know you will not be interrupted and both of you are calm.

Rehearse what you want to say.

Listen to the other person's point of view. This is a good way of showing that you respect and understand the other person.

Use the 'broken record' technique: repeat what you want to say until you think you have been understood.

Learning to be assertive

Many of us are more assertive in certain areas of our lives than in others. For example, we may be very assertive with our brothers and sisters, but not with our friends or teammates. It is very important when we use assertive communication that we show respect for the other person. Learning to be assertive can benefit you in many areas of your life. It can help you to:

- express positive feelings well
- express negative feelings well
- stand up for your rights

 # INDIVIDUAL ACTIVITY

Knowing myself

1. **In each of the areas below, reflect on how assertive you are by ticking the approprriate box.**

	Excellent	Very good	Good	Average	Poor
1. Expressing your feelings					
Telling someone you appreciate them	☐	☐	☐	☐	☐
Giving compliments	☐	☐	☐	☐	☐
Receiving compliments	☐	☐	☐	☐	☐
Starting conversations	☐	☐	☐	☐	☐
2. Expressing negative feelings					
Showing that you are annoyed	☐	☐	☐	☐	☐
Showing that you are hurt	☐	☐	☐	☐	☐
Showing that you are sorry	☐	☐	☐	☐	☐
3. Standing up for your rights					
Making complaints	☐	☐	☐	☐	☐
Refusing requests; saying no	☐	☐	☐	☐	☐
Giving your opinion	☐	☐	☐	☐	☐
Refusing to be put down	☐	☐	☐	☐	☐

2. **Now think about an area of your life where you could be more assertive and how you would go about it. Write about it.**

An area of my life in which I could be more assertive:

_____

How I will be more assertive:

_____

_____

_____

Being safe   Using language

INDIVIDUAL ACTIVITY

Below are definitions of different types of symptoms related to drug use. Read the definitions and then, from the options given in the box, write the drug term next to its definition.

| Tolerance | Physical dependence | Withdrawal |
| Overdose | . | Addiction |

TERM	DESCRIPTION
	This develops when a user gets used to taking a drug and they need higher doses to get the same effects or even to feel normal.
	When a person needs the drug to function normally. Absence of the drug can cause physical symptoms such as constipation, tremors, cramps, sweating, etc.
	An overwhelming and uncontrollable desire to use a drug on a continuous basis. A person is so used to having this drug, they can't function without it even though it can be harmful to them.
	The symptoms that occur when a person stops taking a drug that they have been taking for a while.
	When too much of a drug is taken at once. Illness or death may result.

Drug misuse

Drug misuse is the use of any legal or illegal drug that causes damage to the user's life, including their mental or physical health, their relationships and their ability to function in society.

Being safe;
Being healthy

Learning
with others

GROUP ACTIVITY

As a group, write down as many consequences of drug misuse as you can think of under the headings below.

FAMILY

SCHOOL

DRUGS

RELATIONSHIPS

LEGAL

FINANCIAL

SOCIETY

LEARNING KEEPSAKE

Three things I have learned in this lesson are:

1. _____

2. _____

3. _____

As a result of what I have learned about the effect of drugs, I will:

_____

_____

_____

As a result of this lesson, I will:

_____

_____

_____

_____ has shared this Learning Keepsake with me _____

Name of student

Parent's/Guardian's signature

LESSON 21

Alcohol and its Effects

Learning outcomes: 2.5, 2.6

responsible connected resilient aware

By the end of this lesson you will:

- know more about the effects of alcohol
- recognise the benefits of not drinking
- make more informed decisions about using alcohol
- recognise the skills needed to resist the pressure to drink

KEYWORD

Alcohol

USEFUL WEBSITES

www.drugs.ie Provides drug and alcohol information and support.

www.drinkaware.ie Provides facts on alcohol use in Ireland.

www.barnardos.ie/resources/young-people/drugs-alcohol Provides support and resources for young people experiencing issues with alcohol, themselves or in the home.

www.askaboutalcohol.ie Provides support and advice on alcohol use for individuals or families experiencing alcohol issues.

In Ireland we have a culture of drinking. There is immense pressure on young people to drink alcohol, even from a young age.

Thinking critically

Reading with understanding

INDIVIDUAL ACTIVITY

1. Tick 'Yes' or 'No' to the following statements.

STATEMENT	YES	NO
Have you seen alcohol advertised at sporting events?	☐	☐
Can you name five alcoholic beverages?	☐	☐
Have you seen alcohol being used on sad occasions?	☐	☐
Have you seen movies which portray drinking as a fun thing to do?	☐	☐
Have you ever been in a pub?	☐	☐
Have you seen alcohol in the TV shows you watch?	☐	☐

2. Now read the article below and answer the questions that follow.

Faced with the sober reality of a drunken night out with our teens

As the commuters queued for the buses to go home, the teenagers began to queue to get into the nightclubs around town. At half past six on a busy city street, the barriers went up outside one of the clubs to keep order amongst the youngsters who were celebrating the results of their Junior Cert.

First in line are the boys, with their spiked-up hair and pastel-coloured T-shirts. They are then joined by their girlfriends, who are whooping and shouting with joy at the results they received earlier on in the day. After a few minutes, a small boy, who looks no more than eleven, joins them. He hugs all the girls in the group, who are twice the height of him. But then one of them announces: 'You'd better sober up, or they won't let you in.' One of the T-shirt-clad boys urinates against the newsagents' wall, while another young boy slowly grinds against his girlfriend and then leans against her as they wait for the nightclub to open. Yet another teen takes a long sip out of his can of Dutch Gold, oblivious to the bouncers on the door.

Later, across town, where a non-alcoholic disco is well under way, there is a controlled atmosphere as the Gardaí maintain a presence around the disco. Around fifty teenage boys squeeze their heads through the closed gates like caged animals in the zoo, desperately trying to get in to see the mini-skirted young girls who wait for them on the inside. The disco is full and the bouncers are no longer letting anyone else in. Demand for the event is so strong that tickets have actually been forged for it. One of the bouncers displays his find; they look so close to the real thing that it's almost impossible to tell the difference.

It's a story that we have become accustomed to in the last few years: teenagers are hanging out in non-alcoholic discos, but they're going into them inebriated. While we should never become immune to the sight of a drunken teenager, it's a sad fact that it simply isn't that shocking any more. We shrug our shoulders and say to each other that it wasn't like that in our day. However, when I was faced with the cold reality of what can happen, it's not so easy to adopt such a blasé attitude.

At 9 p.m., the time when most people are just setting out on their night out, the Junior Cert celebrations are already in full swing on another central street. I come across two young girls sitting on the steps near the bus station. Originally I intended to ask them how they had done in their exams and how they were celebrating, but after the first few seconds it was clear that this didn't matter to either of them. One of them is sitting with her head lolling from side to side as she starts to cry. Her friend, who is sober, is fighting back the tears. I had come across the two girls mid-debate over a ruined night, one too drunk to move, too drunk to think, too drunk to protect herself. The drunk girl wants to stay around for another two hours. 'How long does it take to sober up?' she asks me pleadingly. She tells me that she had been drinking gin and vodka. Her friend adds that sometimes this had been with Coke, sometimes straight. She hadn't been allowed into the nightclub because she was too drunk and her sober friend had drawn the short straw by staying with her. A few hundred yards away, the rest of their friends are partying away in the basement of a hotel, oblivious as the two young girls sit on the steps. The drunk girl had gone out to celebrate her Junior Cert results. She was promised a new phone if she did well but now, coming home in this state, she isn't sure if she's going to get it. This was the first time she had been drinking, she tells me.

As I try to persuade the girls to ring one of their mothers, a young man, a few years older, sits down on the step beside them. 'I have a boyfriend,' one of them immediately objects, but this man doesn't care. Seeing two young girls on the steps, he sees an opportunity to pounce and he takes it. 'I'm not going anywhere,' he says, as he becomes increasingly aggressive. A group of his friends stroll by, but he remains, with no interest in what the rest of his friends are doing, just in trying to sidle up to the girls. Then he offers the drunk girl some 'water' he is holding in a Volvic bottle. In her drunken state, she reaches out to take it until I intervene. Increasingly annoyed that his plans were being foiled, he stands up and delivers a barrage of abuse before eventually moving on.

There is no one else on the streets, no one who could have helped them. As soon as he leaves, the girl begins to vomit, the clear liquid pouring out of her lipstick-smudged mouth. Her mascara starts to run, leaving black tear marks on her face. 'I'm so sorry,' she repeats over and over to her friend. 'I'm sorry I ruined your night. Please don't ring my mum. Wait with me until twelve.' Eventually, we ring her mother, who fortunately is just a ten-minute drive away. She pulls her car in across the road, marches over and hoists her daughter off the ground. Trying to stand up, she slips in her own vomit. The friend is left on her own; her friends don't have their phones, she tells me. I bring her down to the nightclub where her friends are, only to find the doors are shut. After I persuade one of the bouncers to let my 'little sister' in, she thankfully rejoins them. Meanwhile, her friend is on the drive home with her mother, who barely even acknowledged my presence as a stranger assisting her daughter. And the only apology she made was to the friend whose night was ruined. Perhaps she didn't realise that it could have been not just their nights, but their lives, that were ruined that night.

(*Source: adapted from* The Sunday Independent)

(a) Do you think this article is realistic? Give reasons for your answer.

(b) Can you identify risky behaviour in this article?

(c) Why might some young people choose to drink alcohol?

(d) Using the information in the article as a prompt, list all the possible negative effects of drinking alcohol.

(e) What would help young people resist the pressure to drink alcohol? In your answer include the personal and social skills they may need.

3. Now fill in the table below regarding your own feelings on alcohol by ticking 'Agree', 'Disagree' or 'Don't Know' in relation to the statements given.

	Agree	Disagree	Don't know
The drinking age limit should be reduced.	☐	☐	☐
Getting drunk is stupid – you just make a fool of yourself.	☐	☐	☐
Young people drink because there is nothing else to do.	☐	☐	☐
Learning about the effects of alcohol is pointless – young people will drink no matter what they are told.	☐	☐	☐
Having friends who drink means you are more likely to drink.	☐	☐	☐
I have the skills to resist the pressure to drink.	☐	☐	☐
I am aware of the risks of underage drinking.	☐	☐	☐
I'll wait until the legal age before I drink.	☐	☐	☐

The benefits of not drinking

By deciding not to drink you are choosing:

✔ to be in control of what you do and what you say

✔ not to put yourself in dangerous or risky situations

✔ to avoid potentially embarrassing or bad experiences

✔ to avoid lowering your inhibitions to a point where you could make poor decisions which could impact your life forever

✔ not to waste money on alcohol

✔ not to break the law

✔ to be healthy and not to fill your body with empty calories

✔ not to impair the development of your brain

✔ not to suffer from crippling hangovers

✔ to allow your body to perform at its best (be that in sports, music, academically, etc.)

Contributing to making the world a better place

A government health agency has come to your school. They want you to devise a national campaign to promote non-drinking amongst teenagers. As a group, come up with a campaign to:

- advise teenagers on how to say no to alcohol
- provide information on the benefits of saying no
- communicate the unglamorous side of drinking
- promote the positive effects of non-drinking

Include a catchy slogan for your campaign, e.g. 'Drinking isn't cool, it makes you act like a fool!'

LEARNING KEEPSAKE

Three things I have learned in this lesson are:

1. _____
2. _____
3. _____

Something that helped me learn in this lesson was:

_____
_____
_____

As a result of this lesson, I will:

_____
_____
_____

_____ has shared this Learning Keepsake with me _____

Name of student   *Parent's/Guardian's signature*

LESSON 22

Cannabis and its Effects

Learning outcomes: 2.5, 2.6, 4.7

responsible connected resilient aware

By the end of this lesson you will:

→ be aware of the health, social and legal implications of using cannabis

→ be able to identify reasons why cannabis should be avoided

 KEYWORDS

Cannabis

Depressant

Dependence

 USEFUL WEBSITE

www.drugs.ie Provides drug information and support.

In Lesson 20 we learned that cannabis is both a depressant and hallucinogen. Cannabis is a very harmful drug and can have very serious effects on both our physical and mental health. This lesson will highlight the personal, social and legal consequences of cannabis use and help you make informed decisions.

Making considered decisions

INDIVIDUAL ACTIVITY

What do you know about cannabis? Tick 'True', 'False' or 'Unsure' in relation to each statement.

	True	False	Unsure
Cannabis is not like other drugs – it is completely safe to take because it is naturally grown.	☐	☐	☐
Cannabis can affect your brain.	☐	☐	☐
Smoking cannabis is not as bad for your health as smoking cigarettes.	☐	☐	☐
Cannabis is the most widely used illegal drug in Ireland.	☐	☐	☐
If you use cannabis, you are not really harming anyone, only yourself.	☐	☐	☐
Cannabis can be detected in a person's urine for up to 28 days after use.	☐	☐	☐
Gardaí have no way of knowing if a driver has used cannabis.	☐	☐	☐
You can become addicted to cannabis.	☐	☐	☐
Cannabis use only has pleasant effects.	☐	☐	☐
It is illegal to grow, produce, supply or possess cannabis for medical or non-medical use.	☐	☐	☐
A person with a drug conviction for cannabis will be refused a visa for a number of countries, including the USA.	☐	☐	☐
You can be arrested for 'supplying' drugs, including cannabis, even if you did not get paid for giving them to someone.	☐	☐	☐

What is cannabis?

Cannabis is a variety of plant. The potency of cannabis is usually expressed in terms of its THC (tetrahydrocannabinol) content. THC is the ingredient in cannabis responsible for its euphoric effect. Slang names for cannabis include marijuana, pot, grass and weed.

Cannabis users can experience mood-altering effects. The precise effects of cannabis on a person can depend on a number of factors, including:

- the strength of the cannabis
- the length of time it has been stored
- the amount that has been used
- the way it is taken
- the experience, mood and expectations of the user

Different types of cannabis

Drug products made from the various species of cannabis plant vary enormously in their THC content. The three types are: cannabis resin, herbal cannabis and cannabis oil.

Cannabis resin

Commonly referred to as hash, it is a soft black or brown lump that looks like a small stock cube. It is scraped down to a powder for use.

Herbal cannabis

Also called grass, marijuana, pot, weed or (in its stronger form) skunk, herbal cannabis looks like dried herbs.

Cannabis oil

The least common and the most powerful form of cannabis. Also called hash oil.

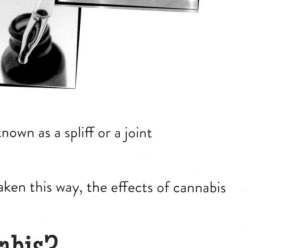

How is cannabis taken?

People take cannabis in a few different ways:

- mixed with tobacco and rolled in a homemade cigarette known as a spliff or a joint
- smoked using a pipe called a bong
- mixed into drinks or baked into cakes or cookies. When taken this way, the effects of cannabis can be more difficult to predict or to control.

What are the effects of using cannabis?

Short-term effects

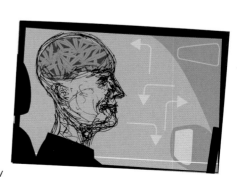

- Increased heart rate and lowered blood pressure
- Weakened short-term memory and learning abilities. Even simple arithmetic skills can be disrupted for 24 hours after a high.
- Increased appetite (sometimes called the 'munchies')
- Inability to perform complex tasks such as driving or using machinery
- May cause feelings of anxiety, suspicion, confusion, panic and paranoia

Long-term effects

- Regular cannabis use can lead to an increased risk of the mental illness schizophrenia in vulnerable people.

- Cannabis use can result in fertility problems for both men and women.

- The smoke and tar from smoking it in a joint impairs lung function.

- Regular users of cannabis may experience lack of motivation or ambition. Research shows that regular cannabis use increases the likelihood of the user dropping out of school.

- Cannabis can affect the way the brain works. Regular, heavy use makes it difficult to learn and concentrate. Heavy users perform poorly in exams.

- Smoking cannabis can put pressure on the heart, which increases heart rate, and can affect blood pressure, which can be especially harmful for those with heart disease.

- Smoking cannabis with tobacco during pregnancy has been linked to increased risk of low birth weight, premature birth and higher risk of miscarriage, as the baby receives less oxygen through the placenta.

Most young teenagers have no interest in taking drugs. Sometimes people take drugs simply because an opportunity arises and they may feel awkward, pressurised or embarrassed about saying no. Have the confidence to make your own decision and say no.

PAIR ACTIVITY

Learning with others

Reading with understanding

Read the story below and answer the questions that follow.

When cannabis takes hold

Aaron is in fifth year. He is the second eldest in his family and has one older brother and two younger sisters. His father works nights and his mother is a healthcare assistant. Aaron is a very bright young man. He coasted through primary school and worked hard in First Year. But midway through Second Year, his work began to deteriorate noticeably and he started to fall behind. At the end of Second Year, his parents were informed that his work was slipping and that many of the teachers had observed that Aaron was often tired, withdrawn and uninterested. He appeared to have lost all motivation.

His mother also began to notice that he was acting very differently at home. She decided to speak to him but he insisted everything was fine. She pleaded with him, and eventually he told her that he had been smoking hash, that he had never really intended to but that his friends were doing it, so he did it so that he wouldn't look stupid or pathetic in front of them. His parents were upset but he assured them he wasn't addicted and that he would stop.

A few months later, Aaron's parents discovered a rather large supply of hash in his bedroom, and when they confronted him he admitted that he was supplying a few friends but that it wasn't a big deal. His parents told him that it had to stop and grounded him.

One evening a few days later, his parents discovered that Aaron wasn't at home when he should have been, and his mother soon realised that a considerable sum of money was missing from her wallet. Aaron didn't come home until late that night, and when he did, he said he had only been out with his friends and denied taking any money from his mother's purse.

Aaron's behaviour continued to get worse; he was skipping school, staying out very late and avoiding his parents. Then one evening there was a knock on the door. One of Aaron's younger sisters answered it, and was greeted by two rough-looking men who asked for Aaron. She told her mother, while Aaron hid in his room, and when his mother came looking for him, asking whether he knew them and what they could possibly want, he begged her to lie and to get rid of them. The men were angry and told Aaron's mother that he owed them €300 and if he didn't come up with the money, there would be trouble. Aaron's parents didn't know what to do. They gave him the money to pay the men, and again made him promise to stop using drugs and to get his act together.

1. Do you think this story is realistic? Why?

_____

_____

2. What was Aaron like before he started using cannabis?

_____

_____

3. Why did Aaron start using cannabis?

_____

_____

4. How do you think his drug use has affected his family?

_____

_____

5. What do you think will happen if he continues to use drugs?

_____

_____

6. What do you think will happen if he stops using drugs?

_____

_____

Knowing myself

Being social

INDIVIDUAL ACTIVITY

On the road below, write in your date of birth, and then write the initials of the friends you have had throughout your life. When you have done that, circle all the people you are still friendly with from primary school. Then answer the questions that follow.

1. Are there any friends you have been friends with for a long time?

_____

2. Write down three qualities you admire in these friends.

_____

3. Have your friendships changed? If so, why do you think that is?

_____

Reasons why friendships change

People drift apart.

One person treats the other badly.

People begin to see unacceptable flaws in the other person.

Somebody changes schools.

Somebody moves away.

A disagreement leads to people falling out.

People change so friendships also change.

There is a lack of trust because of gossip.

People can develop new interests and hobbies and make new friends.

They were not real or loyal friends in the first place.

When friendship goes wrong

Friendships can end for lots of different reasons. If a friendship isn't working, take some time to think and be honest with yourself. Ask yourself these questions:

● Does the friendship make me feel bad about myself?

● Do I enjoy spending time with this person?

● Does the friendship upset me more than it makes me happy?

It can be very difficult to lose a friend. Only you will know if the person and the friendship is worth another chance. Your friend may not know how much they are upsetting you, so try to use your assertive communication skills to let your friend know how you feel.

● Trust your instinct and don't let anyone pressurise you into something that makes you uncomfortable. If you don't want to do something, just say no.

● Let your friend know when their behaviour is unkind and they are upsetting you. Use 'I' statements rather than blaming statements, e.g. 'I feel hurt when you make fun of me in front of others.'

● If you are very upset by your friend's words or actions, talk to a trusted adult or friend about the situation.

Sometimes, for whatever reason, the issues cannot be resolved. An unhealthy or toxic friendship is bad for your wellbeing. If you can't improve the relationship, you should think about ending the friendship. Depending on the situation, there are several ways of ending a toxic friendship.

● Try putting distance between yourself and the friend by spending more time on other pursuits or with other people. In this way, the friendship might simply fizzle out.

● Sometimes it might be necessary to end the friendship directly. This will be difficult to do and you might feel guilty. However, if your friend is bullying you or pressurising you into doing something dangerous, your first duty is to yourself. It will be a difficult thing to do, but the benefits will be long-term and it will be better for you in the end.

Co-operating/
Respecting difference

Using
language

1. In groups, discuss and then answer the following questions:

(a) Give three reasons why a friendship should end.

_____

_____

_____

(b) Give three ways you could resolve a broken friendship.

_____

_____

_____

(c) How would you end a friendship respectfully?

_____

_____

_____

2. Your teacher will now assign one of the scenarios below to each group. In your group, read the scenario and discuss the questions that follow. Choose a reporter to give your group's feedback to the rest of the class.

Scenario 1

Alan is planning on skipping school. He keeps pressuring Brian to come with him. Brian doesn't want to but Alan keeps pestering and teasing him about it so Brian goes out of his way to avoid meeting him.

1. What is the issue in this friendship? _____

_____

2. Can the issue be resolved, and can the friendship be saved? Why? _____

_____

3. What should Brian do next? _____

_____

Scenario 2

Kerry and Ella are best friends. Ella has a new boyfriend. She now spends very little time with Ella. Sometimes Kerry does not reply to Ella's texts. Ella is worried about their friendship.

1. What is the issue in this friendship? _____

_____

2. Can the issue be resolved, and can the friendship be saved? Why? _____

_____

3. What should Kerry do next?_____

_____

Scenario 3

Yvette and Trish have been friends for a long time. Whenever they are with their larger group of friends, Yvette keeps trying to embarrass Trish by bringing up embarrassing things Trish did when they were younger. When they are alone, Trish asks Yvette not to do this as it makes her feel bad, but Yvette continues to ridicule Trish when others are around.

1. What is the issue in this friendship? _____

_____

2. Can the issue be resolved, and can the friendship be saved? Why? _____

_____

3. What should Trish do next? _____

_____

Scenario 4

Lynn is sure about one thing: she wants to be a doctor when she leaves school. She studies hard to achieve good grades. In contrast, Lynn's best friend, Kate, is unsure what she wants to do after school and is getting sick and tired of Lynn spending all her time studying. She thinks Lynn just isn't fun anymore. Lynn's friend, Ben, tells her that Kate has been talking about her behind her back, calling her a swot and a bore and saying that the only reason Lynn is doing well in her exams is because her dad is loaded and is getting her grinds. Lynn is furious. She can't believe that her friend would say such things.

1. What is the issue in this friendship? _____

_____

2. Can the issue be resolved, and can the friendship be saved? Why? _____

_____

3. What should Lynn do next? _____

_____

Scenario 5

Derek and Sam had an argument before the summer holidays. They haven't spoken since. When they returned to school after the summer break, their SPHE teacher paired them to work together on their CBA. They both find this situation very awkward.

1. What is the issue in this friendship? _____

_____

2. Can the issue be resolved, and can the friendship be saved? Why? _____

_____

3. What could they do next? _____

_____

Scenario 6

Clem and Jamie are great friends. Recently, Clem told Jamie that he is feeling quite down because his parents are breaking up. Clem asked Jamie to promise not to tell anybody. After training, when they are packing up to go home, another teammate sits beside Clem and says, 'Jamie told me about your parents. I hope you are doing okay.'

1. What is the issue in this friendship? _____

_____

2. Can the issue be resolved, and can the friendship be saved? Why? _____

_____

3. What should Clem do next? _____

_____

LEARNING KEEPSAKE

Three things I have learned in this lesson are:

1. _____
2. _____
3. _____

Something that helped me learn in this lesson was:

_____

_____

_____

As a result of this lesson, I will:

_____

_____

_____

_____ has shared this Learning Keepsake with me _____

Name of student   *Parent's/Guardian's signature*

LESSON 24 — Peer Pressure and Other Influences

Learning outcomes: 2.5, 3.4

responsible   connected   aware

By the end of this lesson you will:
- ➨ have analysed how young people are influenced by their friends
- ➨ have identified strategies for dealing with peer pressure

KEYWORDS

Peers

Pressure

Authority

Who influences us?

To 'influence' means to affect the thoughts, actions and behaviour of others. Young people are most influenced by their family and their peer group. 'Peers' are people of similar age to you who share the same experiences and interests as you. 'Peer pressure' refers to the powerful influence people your own age can have over the decisions you make. Peer pressure can be spoken or unspoken, positive or negative.

1 Spoken peer pressure is when people say certain things to someone else to try and persuade them to do something. You may be pressured into doing something you're uncomfortable with, such as shoplifting, doing drugs, smoking or drinking.

2 Unspoken peer pressure is often harder to recognise. It is when you feel pressure to act a certain way, even though no one is telling you to, e.g. if your friends are all doing something, you may feel you have to do the same thing as you don't want to be different. Unspoken peer pressure can be hard to resist because you are standing up to a personal feeling rather than another person. Note that unspoken peer pressure is not always deliberate.

Learning with others

GROUP ACTIVITY

1. In groups, brainstorm sources of peer pressure for someone your age. Remember to include some positive as well as negative sources.

SOURCES OF PEER PRESSURE

2. Read the six scenarios below and answer the questions that follow.

Scenario 1

Pamela is new to the class. She hasn't made any new friends yet. She overhears a group of girls talking about pranking the teacher. Before the teacher enters the room, one of the girls shouts across the room to Pamela telling her to wet the teacher's chair. Pamela really wants to make friends but she doesn't want to do something like this.

1. Is this deliberate peer pressure?_____

_____

2. Is the pressure spoken or unspoken?_____

_____

3. How would you feel in this situation?_____

_____

Scenario 2

Tom's friends are always messing in class. He knows that lately he has fallen behind in Irish. He is really trying to pay more attention in class, but doesn't want to take part and answer the teacher's questions in case his friends think he is a nerd.

1. Is this deliberate peer pressure?_____

_____

2. Is the pressure spoken or unspoken?_____

_____

3. How would you feel in this situation?_____

_____

Scenario 3

Rachel loves hockey and is really talented at it. More often than not she makes the starting team. Her friend, Maria, is good offensively but finds playing defensively really difficult. Rachel decides to send Maria some videos she has found online about how to improve her defensive skills, and tells her she will stay back after training with her to do some extra skills work, because she knows Maria would really like to make the starting team more often.

1. Is this deliberate peer pressure?_____

_____

2. Is the pressure spoken or unspoken?_____

_____

3. How would you feel in this situation?_____

_____

Scenario 4

Jed doesn't like maths and finds it very difficult. Jed's best friend, Mike, is a straight-A student who loves maths. When the teacher puts them together for pair work, Mike encourages Jed to look at the examples in the book and to figure out the maths problems line by line. Mike tells Jed that this is how he became good at maths in the first place.

1. Is this deliberate peer pressure?_____

_____

2. Is the pressure spoken or unspoken?_____

_____

3. How would you feel in this situation?_____

Scenario 5

Shauna has made friends with a new group at school. They often post negative comments under the feeds of students from other schools in the area, and are encouraging Shauna to do the same. Shauna really does not want to as she doesn't like the idea of upsetting other people, and knows it could just as easily be her another time.

1. Is this deliberate peer pressure?_____

_____

2. Is the pressure spoken or unspoken?_____

_____

3. How would you feel in this situation?_____

_____

Scenario 6

Joe is going to the teenage disco. Before the disco, he meets up in Conor's house. While they are getting ready, Conor takes out a bottle of vodka. He pours a glass for himself and one for Joe.

1. Is this deliberate peer pressure?_____

_____

2. Is the pressure spoken or unspoken?_____

_____

3. How would you feel in this situation?_____

_____

Resisting peer pressure

Negative peer pressure can get you into trouble or even danger, e.g. peer pressure to get involved in illegal activities such as drinking alcohol or taking drugs. It is important for you to recognise negative peer pressure and to learn how to resist it. Sometimes resisting peer pressure may not be easy and it takes a little practice. Rather than simply going along with the crowd, think about whether the activity being suggested or forced upon you is something you really want to do.

Resisting peer pressure can be difficult for some people because:

→ Peer pressure can make you feel very uncomfortable.

→ You feel pressurised to do something just because others are doing it.

→ You may not want to hurt someone else's feelings.

→ You want to be liked and don't want to lose friends.

→ You want to feel accepted.

→ You don't want to stand out or be different.

→ You don't want to be left out or rejected.

→ You don't have the skills to stand up to it.

→ You are afraid of being made fun of.

Tips for resisting negative peer pressure

☞ Know your own mind. Know what is right and what is wrong for you. If you feel uncomfortable in a situation, then you know it's not right – even if your friends are fine with what's going on, it doesn't mean it's right for you.

☞ Be prepared. If you think a situation will be difficult to get out of, plan ahead and have a line prepared to help you resist the pressure – blame your parents if you have to, e.g. 'My father would go mad if he caught me and he always catches me!' Rehearse what you are going to say and stickto it.

☞ Learn to say 'no'. Be confident, stand up straight and say exactly how you feel. A true friend will accept your decision. They will not fall out with you because you don't want to do something.

☞ Walk away. If the situation is dangerous, call an adult to come and get you.

GROUP ACTIVITY

Learning creatively

Performing and presenting

In groups, and using the tips you have just learned for resisting negative peer pressure, role-play the following scenarios, coming up with ways to resist the peer pressure. Then come up with three things that would help you to resist negative peer pressure.

Scenario 1
You are out with your friends when one of them tells you how great vaping is and insists that you should try it.

Scenario 2
You are in town with your friends when one of them picks up a computer game and asks you to slip it into your back pocket while they distract the cashier.

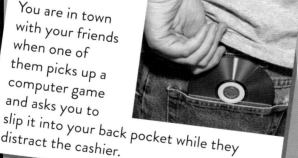

Scenario 3
You are out with your friends when they pull out graffiti cans and start tagging walls in your neighbourhood, handing you the can so that you can do the same.

Three things that would work best for me to resist peer pressure are:

1. _____

2. _____

3. _____

INDIVIDUAL ACTIVITY

Knowing myself

Now that you are aware of some positive and negative examples of peer pressure, read the following statements and tick the ones that apply to you.

STATEMENT	LIKE ME	NOT LIKE ME
You should go along with your friends even if you do not agree with what they are doing.	☐	☐
It is important that you do not stand out from your peers.	☐	☐
You feel embarrassed if you are not allowed to do what your friends are doing.	☐	☐
At times, you find it difficult to stand up for what you believe in.	☐	☐

LEARNING KEEPSAKE

Three things I have learned in this lesson are:

1. _____

2. _____

3. _____

Something that helped me learn in this lesson was:

_____

_____

_____

As a result of this lesson, I will:

_____

_____

_____

_____ has shared this Learning Keepsake with me _____

Name of student   *Parent's/Guardian's signature*

TOPIC 2
The Relationship Spectrum

Managing Relationships

Learning outcome: 3.4

responsible   aware

By the end of this lesson you will:

•+ understand the different relationships in your life

•+ appreciate how to establish and maintain good relationships

KEYWORDS

Relationships

Acquaintances

A relationship involves a special connection between people. As we grow up, we meet many people. Only a few of these encounters will result in relationships or friendships. Some people are happy to be with family and friends and have little or no interest in being in a romantic relationship, while others can't start a relationship quick enough; some people have a wide circle of friends and acquaintances, while others prefer only a few close friends. We are all unique and have different wants, needs, desires and values.

INDIVIDUAL ACTIVITY

Knowing myself

1. You are now going to explore the different relationships in your life. A few relationships will be with people who are close to you and know you very well; others may be acquaintances or people you meet rarely. Place the initials of the people in your life in the appropriate circle:

● The inner circle contains your closest relationships with the people who mean the most to you and who you trust and confide in the most.

● The middle circle contains other casual friends and distant relatives who you see regularly enough but with whom you do not have as close a bond.

● The outer circle will contain people you meet occasionally but do not know very well.

THE OUTER CIRCLE
Acquaintances

THE INTERMEDIATE CIRCLE
Casual friends and relatives

THE INNER CIRCLE
Close family and friends

2. Consider one of the people in your inner circle and answer the following questions:

(a) How does your relationship with someone in the inner circle differ from your relationships with people in the other two circles?

_____

_____

(b) What kind of things would you be comfortable sharing or talking about with people in each circle?

_____

_____

(c) Do you think you need to be careful about which people you share personal information with? Give reasons.

_____

_____

Managing relationships

Relationships can range from healthy to unhealthy to abusive. Healthy relationships require work and effort by everyone involved. Healthy romantic relationships, family relationships or friendships all share the same core values.

Tips for healthy relationships

- ☞ **Communication:** Talk openly, listen to one another, hear each other out.

- ☞ **Practise empathy:** Consider how the other person feels, imagine what the other person is feeling. Put yourself in their shoes.

- ☞ **Compromise:** Be willing to meet half way.

- ☞ **Set boundaries:** Have clear limits on how you want to be treated and how you will treat others. Have a good sense of what is acceptable and what is not, physically, emotionally and verbally.

- ☞ **Encourage:** Support yourself, your goals and the goals of others. Be each other's biggest cheerleader.

- ☞ **Maintain outside friendships:** Don't spend all your time with one person. Make time for other important people in your life, including friends and family members.

- ☞ **Be responsible:** Accept when you are wrong and take ownership.

- ☞ **Trust:** Be open and honest, follow through, don't let the other person down.

- ☞ **Equality:** Treat each other fairly and equally, have a balance in the relationship. Value the other person's opinion and rights.

- ☞ **Be genuine:** Treat others as you would like to be treated, be positive towards others.

 **INDIVIDUAL ACTIVITY**

Managing myself   Being social

Think about someone else in your inner circle. Reflect on your behaviour towards this person. Answer the following statements truthfully by ticking the relevant box.

STATEMENT	ALWAYS	OFTEN	SOMETIMES	NEVER
I speak to this person openly and I am honest with them about my feelings.	☐	☐	☐	☐
When we have a disagreement or they are upset by something they feel I have done, I stay calm and try to listen to their side.	☐	☐	☐	☐
I try to be there for this person as much as I can.	☐	☐	☐	☐
I make time for other people in my life.	☐	☐	☐	☐
I show this person respect.	☐	☐	☐	☐
I am kind to this person.	☐	☐	☐	☐
I admit when I am wrong.	☐	☐	☐	☐
I trust this person.	☐	☐	☐	☐
I encourage this person.	☐	☐	☐	☐

- If you have answered mostly 'always' or 'often', then the chances are that you are trying hard to maintain a healthy relationship. Remember, this activity only focuses on your behaviour. For a relationship to be healthy, both people need to behave in this way.

- If you have answered mostly 'sometimes' or 'never', then the chances are you need to work harder on your relationship to ensure that it is a healthy relationship for you both. Consider using the tips for healthy relationships to maintain or establish a healthy relationship.

LEARNING KEEPSAKE

Three things I have learned in this lesson are:

1. _____

2. _____

3. _____

Something that helped me learn in this lesson was:

_____

_____

_____

As a result of this lesson, I will:

_____

_____

_____

_____ has shared this Learning Keepsake with me _____

Name of student   *Parent's/Guardian's signature*

LESSON 26

Health and Personal Safety

Learning outcome: 3.5

responsible   resilient   aware

By the end of this lesson you will:

• understand relationship difficulties experienced by young people
• appreciate the importance of having boundaries in relationships
• recognise the importance of keeping safe when in a relationship or out socialising

KEYWORDS

Boundaries

Pressures

As you grow up, you might begin to meet, date and explore greater levels of intimacy with someone. This provides teens with the opportunity to develop skills and behaviours for building and maintaining healthy relationships. There is no set time or age at which to start dating; it depends on how much a person wants to date, if they meet anyone they are interested in dating and who is worth dating, or it might be influenced by their values, their culture or their religious background.

INDIVIDUAL ACTIVITY

Knowing myself;
Making considered
decisions

Reading
with
understanding

Read the scenario below and answer the questions that follow.

John is 14 years old. He enjoys sports and spends most of his time playing basketball. He is really happy in school, he does well and is popular in class. Recently, some of his friends have begun going to discos. He doesn't really have any interest in going out just yet. His friends really want him to come along to the next disco, and even though he really doesn't want to go, his friends have been slagging him so much that eventually he decides to go. He is nervous all day; his stomach is in a knot but he doesn't really know why. When he gets to the disco he is very uncomfortable and anxious about what is going to happen. They seem to take it all in their stride. His friends start to slag him about a girl in the class who likes him, pushing him and egging him on to approach her. He doesn't know what to do.

1. Why do you think John's friends pressurise him to go to the disco?

_____

_____

2. Why do you think John was nervous about going?

_____

_____

3. Do you think he should have gone to the disco?

_____

_____

4. Do you think his friends are being good friends?

_____

_____

5. What advice would you give to John?

_____

_____

CLASS DISCUSSION

Discussing/Debating

Knowing your boundaries and staying safe

Beginning a romantic relationship should be fun. You should feel comfortable at all times. Take your time to get to know the other person. It is important to think about what you are ready for and to share your thoughts, expectations and boundaries. It is also important to keep yourself as safe as you can.

Boundaries

Boundaries are invisible barriers between you and another person. Boundaries are important in all relationships as they set out limits beyond which you will not go and behaviours which you will not tolerate in others, e.g. controlling, demanding, critical or manipulative behaviours. Boundaries are important and keep us safe. It is important that you communicate what makes you comfortable or uncomfortable and are able to communicate your boundaries to others.

Here are some phrases you could use:

I am not comfortable about ...

I'd rather not ...

I feel uncomfortable about ...

Yes, I do mind ...

I don't want to ...

I'll think about that ...

I have decided not to ...

Staying safe

When meeting people, either online or in person, knowing and communicating your boundaries is important for your safety.

- If it is your first time meeting, you may want to go out with another couple or in a group.

- Stay where there are other people around.

- Be aware of the effects of alcohol and the risks of sexual activity that may result.

- Know your sexual limits and respect others.

- Be clear about your limits and boundaries with the other person.

- Be honest and don't be afraid to voice your feelings.

- If you decide not to see the person again, be respectful and kind. Communicate your feelings honestly.

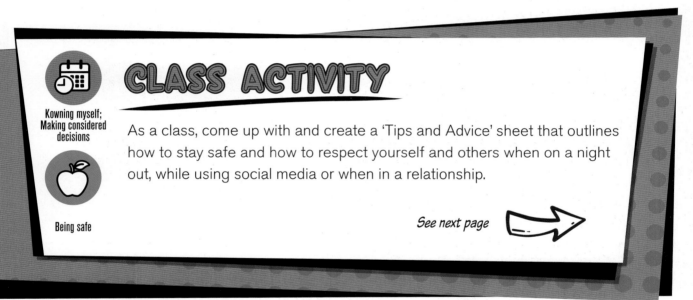

CLASS ACTIVITY

Kowning myself; Making considered decisions

Being safe

As a class, come up with and create a 'Tips and Advice' sheet that outlines how to stay safe and how to respect yourself and others when on a night out, while using social media or when in a relationship.

See next page

In Ireland, the law states that you must be seventeen to consent to (agree to) have sexual intercourse. The age of consent is the same for males and females. It is illegal for anyone under seventeen to have sex. Non-consensual sexual activity at any age is also against the law.

STOP

Tips and Advice on Staying Safe and Respecting Yourself and Others

On a night out

Using social media

In a relationship

LEARNING KEEPSAKE

Three things I have learned in this lesson are:

1. _____

2. _____

3. _____

Something that helped me learn in this lesson was:

_____

_____

_____

As a result of this lesson, I will:

_____

_____

_____

_____ has shared this Learning Keepsake with me _____

Name of student   *Parent's/Guardian's signature*

TOPIC 3
Sexuality, Gender Identity and Sexual Health

LESSON 27
From Conception to Birth

Learning outcome: 3.6

responsible

aware

By the end of this lesson you will:

- know the stages of development from conception to birth
- appreciate the importance of a woman looking after herself before and during pregnancy

KEYWORDS

Conception

Foetus

Contractions

Dilated

Last year you learned about all the different changes that take place in your body that enable you to become a parent one day. You also learned about the story of reproduction. This year you will learn the rest of this story, that of conception to birth. You will also become aware of the health considerations for a women before and during pregnancy.

Thinking critically

In pairs, complete the following cloze text about having a healthy pregnancy and answer the questions that follow.

A woman planning a baby should have a healthy
_____ _____ and _____.
It is important to take _____ _____
before and during pregnancy. This has been shown to reduce the
risk of the baby having _____ _____.
Sources include leafy _____, _____
and _____.
Pregnant women should avoid _____ and
_____. If a woman drinks _____ during
pregnancy, she risks damaging her baby. Sometimes this can
result in _____ and _____ problems
in the baby, called _____ _____
_____. Smoking during pregnancy can cause low
_____ _____ or even _____. A
pregnant woman should consult her doctor before taking any
_____.

During pregnancy certain foods should be avoided:
_____ dairy products, _____ and
_____ _____ could cause food poisoning and harm the
unborn child.

legumes
vegetables
folic acid
shellfish
medication
spina bifida
exercise regime
raw eggs
alcohol (x2)
foetal alcohol syndrome
diet
birth weight
tobacco
mental
physical
unpasteurised
miscarriage
cereals

INDIVIDUAL ACTIVITY

Thinking creatively and critically

Answer the following questions:

1. Write down three things a woman could do to prepare for pregnancy.

    (a) _____

    (b) _____

    (c) _____

2. Why do you think it is important for a woman to take care of her body when she is planning a pregnancy?

   _____

3. List three people who could support a pregnant woman and suggest what kind of support they could offer.

   (a) _____

   (b) _____

   (c) _____

From conception to birth

Conception to week 4

After the woman's egg has been fertilised by the man's sperm, it forms a single cell. This cell first divides into two, then into four, then into eight and so on. The ball of cells moves along the Fallopian tube to the uterus (womb). Once in the uterus, it divides into the embryo and placenta and embeds itself in the lining of the uterus.

Environment

For the duration of the pregnancy the embryo lives inside the uterus. The embryo is protected in a fluid-filled sac called the amniotic sac. The fluid in the amniotic sac is released during childbirth: this is what happens when the waters break.

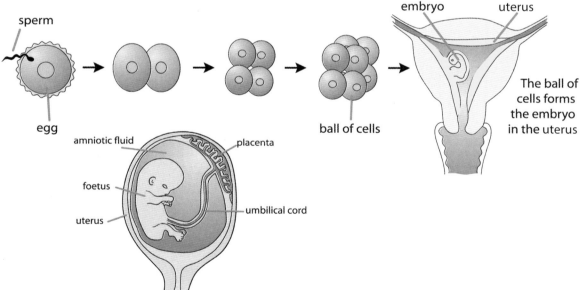

Weeks 5–8

At this stage the embryo is now referred to as a foetus. All the foetus's organs are in place and continue to develop. The face is forming. If the mother were to have an ultrasound now, she would be able to hear the foetus's heartbeat. The arms and legs appear as buds. The foetus is about the size of a five cent coin.

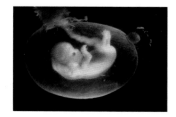

Weeks 9–12

In weeks 9 and 10 the facial features form. The foetus is fully formed by week 12 and will continue to grow for the rest of the pregnancy. The placenta is fully developed, passing oxygen and nutrients from the mother to the foetus and carrying away carbon dioxide and waste via the umbilical cord.

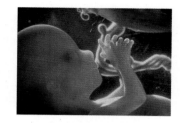

Weeks 13–20

The foetus continues to grow. Movement may be felt by weeks 16–18. By week 18 the eyelashes and eyebrows begin to grow. By week 20 the foetus is now about 11 cm long and its sex can be identified by ultrasound.

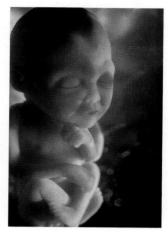

Weeks 21–40

By week 28, the foetus has reached a weight and stage of organ development that would enable it to survive outside the womb with some support – the baby would still need help with breathing and feeding until he/she became more mature.

By week 36, the foetus is more restricted in the uterus and the head settles downwards in preparation for birth.

In the last three weeks the pregnancy reaches full term and the baby can be born at any time now. The baby lies head down waiting for the birth.

The three stages of birth

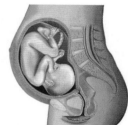

1. **From the start of contractions to fully dilated.**

   - When the baby is ready to be born the mother experiences painful contractions.

   - The contractions cause the neck of the womb to open. This stage of the birth is called labour.

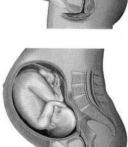

   - When the neck of the womb (called the cervix) is fully dilated – ten centimetres wide – the baby is ready to be born.

   - The waters can break at any time during the birth.

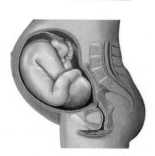

   - There are several different strategies to help the mother through labour pains. These include breathing/relaxation techniques, painkilling injections, epidurals and Entonox (gas and air).

2. From fully dilated to delivery of the baby.

- The baby moves through the birth canal (vagina), aided by the mother's pushing and the powerful contractions.

- When the widest part of the baby's head is delivered, this is known as crowning.

- Once the baby is delivered the umbilical cord is clamped and cut.

- The baby's first cry enables the lungs to inflate with air.

3. Delivery of the placenta.

- After the baby is born, the placenta dislodges itself from the lining of the womb and is expelled by contractions.

- The mother sometimes receives an injection after the baby is born to aid this process.

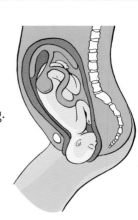

Caesarean section

Caesarean section is when the baby is delivered by cutting the womb through the lower abdomen. This method is performed if there are complications in pregnancy or childbirth, for example in a breech birth (where the baby is coming feet or buttocks first), if the baby is distressed, or if the cervix does not dilate fully.

 INDIVIDUAL ACTIVITY

Evaluating my learning

Test your knowledge of conception and childbirth by completing this crossword.

Across

7 This connects the embryo to the placenta and later forms the baby's belly button. (9, 4)

9 Food and oxygen pass from the mother to the baby through this. (8)

10 This occurs when the widest part of the baby's head is delivered. (8)

11 These occur when the baby is ready to be born. (12)

12 The joining together of the female's egg and the male's sperm. (13)

Down

1 You should take this if you are planning to have a baby. (5, 4)

2 The egg is located here when it is ready to be fertilised. (9, 4)

3 This fluid protects the baby and prevents it from being injured. (8)

4 A normal pregnancy lasts about ...... months. (4)

5 This waste substance passes from the baby to the mother. (6, 7)

6 The baby lives here for the duration of the pregnancy. (4)

8 .... dairy products should be avoided during pregnancy. (13)

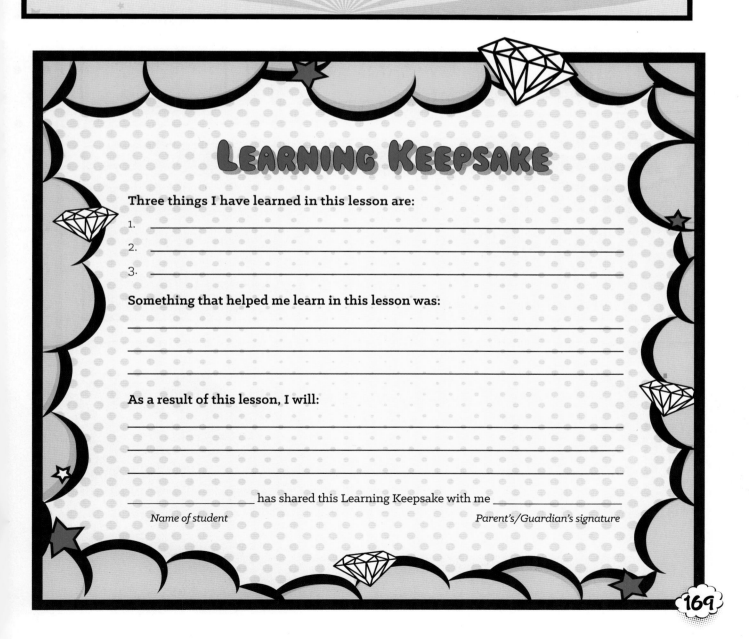

LEARNING KEEPSAKE

Three things I have learned in this lesson are:

1. _____
2. _____
3. _____

Something that helped me learn in this lesson was:

_____
_____
_____

As a result of this lesson, I will:

_____
_____
_____

_____ has shared this Learning Keepsake with me _____

Name of student   *Parent's/Guardian's signature*

LESSON 28
Sexuality, Sexual Identity and Sexual Orientation

Learning outcomes: 1.4, 3.9

responsible

connected

respected

aware

By the end of this lesson you will:

- further understand the language used to talk about sexual orientation and sexual identity
- understand the need for acceptance of self and others
- appreciate the social and personal dimensions of sexual orientation
- identify the way in which your school can create a safe and inclusive environment for LGBTQ+ students

KEYWORDS

Sexual orientation

Gender identity

Coming out

Acceptance

USEFUL WEBSITES

www.lgbt.ie A support and education organisation to help and enhance the lives of LGBTQ+ people in Ireland. **Phone 1890 929 539**.

www.belongto.org Offers support and advice for lesbian, gay, bisexual and transgender young people.

www.teni.ie Transgender Equality Network Ireland (TENI) provides information and support to transgender people and their families.

INDIVIDUAL ACTIVITY

Reflecting on and
evaluating my learning

You learned about the following words and phrases in First Year. Now, in your own words, write what you think they mean.

	YOUR MEANING
Sexual orientation	
Gender identity	
Heterosexual	
Heterosexism	
Homosexual (gay or lesbian)	
Bisexual	
Transgender	
Transition	
Coming out	
Homophobia	

GROUP ACTIVITY

Listening and
expressing myself

As a group, discuss the following statements:

In our school, LGBTQ+ young people always feel safe and are respected.

LGBTQ+ relationships are well represented in advertising.

A young person in an LGBTQ+ relationship can openly express their feelings and identity with friends and family.

A young person in an LGBTQ+ relationship can openly express their feelings and affection for each other in their community.

Acceptance of self and others

Sexuality is much more than sexual feelings or having sex; it involves our relationships with ourselves, those around us and the society in which we live. No matter what our sexual orientation, we all have the same needs, such as physical and emotional intimacy, love, belonging, friendship and commitment. Our sexual identity is an important part, but only one part, of who we are. It is important to explore our feelings and accept our sexuality whether we are straight, gay, lesbian, bisexual, asexual and/or transgender.

Today, Ireland is for the most part an open and diverse society that is increasingly moving towards equality where all people can live freely and be accepted for who they are. We saw this with the Yes vote in the Marriage Equality referendum in 2015. Ireland was the first country to bring in same-sex marriage by means of a 'popular' vote (the public voted on it and decided; in other countries where same-sex marriage is allowed, the government decided on it).

Being able to express your sexuality is very important and should be respected. It is also very important to respect other people's orientation and gender identity. Bullying or judging someone based on their sexual orientation is wrong and should not be tolerated.

We learned in First Year that homophobic bullying or transphobic bullying can affect a person's self-esteem, emotional health and wellbeing. It can also have an effect on their school attendance and grades. People may be a target of this type of bullying because of their sexual orientation or their perceived sexual orientation. Similar to all forms of bullying, homophobic bullying can take the form of name-calling, spreading rumours, or physical, sexual or emotional abuse.

> Sometimes we can contribute to discrimination by saying things that we don't realise have consequences. So bear the following in mind:
> - Do not tease people by saying that they are gay.
> - Do not use the word 'gay' in a negative way, such as when referring to something being stupid and saying, 'That's so gay!'

Stand up for your LGBTQ+ friend

Listening and
expressing myself

GROUP ACTIVITY

Read the scenarios below and, as a group, discuss them using the questions provided.

Scenario 1

Your friend, who is captain of the school rugby team, has confided in you that he is gay. He has told you that he is nervous about coming out to teammates and classmates.

1. Why do you think this boy is nervous about coming out?

2. Would he feel differently if he had the support of others?

3. What can students and staff do to make the school a more accepting place for him to come out?

4. What could you do to help and support him?

Scenario 2

A homophobic slur has been written on the locker door of a student at your school. No one claims responsibility. Most people in the school have seen what has been written on the locker.

1. What effect would this have on LGBTQ+ students in the school?

2. How would this graffiti affect the individual student's wellbeing?

3. What can students and staff do to deal with this situation?

4. What could you do to help and support the student involved.

We have all had and will all have challenging and difficult times in our lives. The ability to talk honestly and openly with someone we trust is an important skill in looking after our wellbeing. This is the first step towards getting support and feeling better.

LEARNING KEEPSAKE

Three things I have learned in this lesson are:

1. _____

2. _____

3. _____

Something that helped me learn in this lesson was:

_____

_____

_____

As a result of this lesson, I will:

_____

_____

_____

_____ has shared this Learning Keepsake with me _____

Name of student   *Parent's/Guardian's signature*

MEET THE CHALLENGE
Strand 3 Topic 3
1. A SLIDESHOW ON PRE-NATAL DEVELOPMENT AND BIRTH

Learning outcome: 3.6

Working in pairs, design a slide show on the stages in pre-natal development and birth. Include:

○ information on fertility

○ a timeline of the baby's development

○ the stages of birth

○ pictures, animations and other visual displays

At the end of your slide show, outline further information that you feel is important for expectant parents, including information on the responsibilities of parenthood.

MEET THE CHALLENGE
Strand 3 Topic 3
2. LGBTQ+ ACCEPTANCE STAND

Learning outcomes: 1.1, 1.2, 1.3, 1.4, 1.8, 1.9, 2.3, 2.10, 3.9

To promote inclusion and support for LGBTQ+ students, your class has decided to run a stand giving out literature on LGBTQ+ acceptance and promoting LGBTQ+ inclusion at your school during a school event. Your class will need to break into four groups responsible for different aspects of running a successful stand.

Group 1: Design and set up

○ Plan the design and the layout of the stand.

○ Decorate the stand with an LGBTQ+ theme.

○ Set up the stand on the day of the event.

Group 2: Research supports

○ Research supports that are available to people who are struggling with their sexual identity.

○ Make business cards for the stand that will give names and contact details for these support services and a brief outline of the services that they offer.

Group 3: Promotion of strong, positive anti-homophobic bullying message

○ Promote the message 'Stand up against homophobic bullying' using posters, leaflets, videos, etc. that can work at a display stand.

○ Promote a message of inclusion for students who may identify as LGBTQ+, e.g. information on 'what is homophobic bullying?' and what young people can do if they encounter homophobic bullying.

Group 4: Stand promotors

○ Responsible for running the stand on the day of the event.

○ Before the event, this group will need to research the different areas of LGBTQ+ and have a knowledge of the correct terminology around this topic.

○ Work with the other groups to gain an understanding of what information they are contributing to the stand.

○ Be prepared to talk to students who come to visit the stand and who may have questions or need further information.

MY MENTAL HEALTH

STRAND 4

TOPIC 1
Positive Mental Health

Self-Confidence

Learning outcome: 4.2

responsible   connected   resilient   aware

By the end of this lesson you will:
→ have improved your skills of raising your self-esteem
→ recognise that our thoughts, feelings and behaviours are linked

KEYWORDS

Self-esteem

Self-confidence

Self-esteem and self-confidence

Self-esteem is all about how much you value yourself and how you feel about yourself overall. People with healthy self-esteem feel good about themselves, appreciate their own worth, and are proud of themselves. People with low self-esteem may be less able to recognise their qualities and accomplishments.

Self-esteem and self-confidence are linked, but they are not the same: self-confidence is more to do with how you feel about your capabilities. You can develop your capabilities to improve both self-esteem and self-confidence.

Learning to be self-confident

As a teenager, you will have many different thoughts and feelings about different aspects of your life. These may be thoughts about:

● how you see yourself

● how you judge what you do

● your views on the future

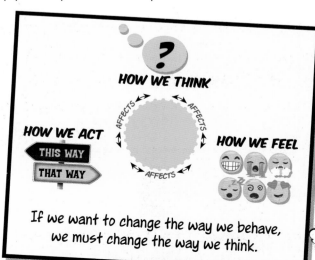

HOW WE THINK

HOW WE ACT
THIS WAY
THAT WAY

AFFECTS   AFFECTS

AFFECTS

HOW WE FEEL

If we want to change the way we behave, we must change the way we think.

177

The thoughts we have about ourselves can affect our self-confidence. Our thoughts can be positive, for example, 'I played well in the game today', or they can be negative, for example, 'I played really badly today'. We can't stop these negative thoughts but we can learn to manage them. Learning how to challenge unhelpful thoughts can increase our self-confidence and make us more resilient.

INDIVIDUAL ACTIVITY

Knowing myself

Read the unhelpful thoughts on the left and write a helpful thought to challenge each one.

UNHELPFUL THOUGHT	HELPFUL THOUGHT
I'll never be good at this.	If I keep practising, I will improve bit by bit.
This is too hard.	
The last time I tried this, I failed, so I am wasting my time even trying.	
Everyone can do this except me.	
I'm always making mistakes.	
The day is completely ruined.	

Being confident

CLASS ACTIVITY

Our thoughts can have a powerful impact on how we feel and how we act in a situation. When we use helpful ways of thinking, we can change how we feel and how we act in a situation. Read the following two reactions to a similar situation and, as a class, discuss the consequences of each reaction.

Response 1: Rory

Rory is walking down the street. He passes a group of students from his school who he is not very friendly with. One of the group makes a nasty comment about him and they all laugh.

What is he thinking?
'What they said must be true.'
'Everyone must think this about me.'

What does he do?
He puts his head down.
He gets angry with his brother when he gets home.
He goes straight up to his room.

How is he feeling?
Sad
Embarrassed
Paranoid

Response 2: Jack

A few minutes later, Jack, Rory's friend, walks down the same street. As he passes the group they make a similar nasty remark, and they all laugh.

What is he thinking?
'I don't care what other people think.'
'They are putting me down to make themselves feel better.'
'They are just trying to impress their friends.'

What does he do?
He brushes it off.
He thinks about his friends and other people who make him feel good about himself.
He forgets about it.

How is he feeling?
Confident
Assured
Positive

179

Knowing myself

Being confident

INDIVIDUAL ACTIVITY

As you can see, there are two − or more − reactions to every situation, and how we think can influence how we respond. Read the following scenario and complete the flow chart.

Scenario

Your teacher gives you back an exam. You have failed.

UNHELPFUL RESPONSE

What are you thinking?

What are you doing?

How are you feeling?

HELPFUL RESPONSE

What are you thinking?

What are you doing?

How are you feeling?

REMEMBER

- Unhelpful thinking can make us feel bad about ourselves, lower our self-esteem and prevent us reaching our potential.
- Helpful thinking encourages us to feel better about ourselves, to be resilient and to work towards achieving our goals.
- Just because we have an unhelpful thought does not make it true.
- Most of us are very good at zoning in on our failures or shortcomings. In doing this we fail to recognise the good things about ourselves.
- When you have an unhelpful thought, ask yourself, 'Would I say this to a friend?'
- Talking positively to ourselves helps us to become more self-confident.

Knowing
myself

Being
confident

INDIVIDUAL ACTIVITY

Design a poster for your bedroom wall to remind yourself of your positive qualities. The poster should include:

- something positive about yourself

- something positive you have achieved

- things or people who make you feel good about yourself

- something positive you would like to achieve

- a compliment you received in the past that made you feel good

- one thing for which you are grateful

LEARNING KEEPSAKE

Three things I have learned in this lesson are:

1. _____
2. _____
3. _____

Something that helped me learn in this lesson was:

_____
_____
_____

As a result of this lesson, I will:

_____
_____
_____

_____ has shared this Learning Keepsake with me _____

Name of student   *Parent's/Guardian's signature*

Positive and Negative Influences

Learning outcomes: 2.2, 4.2

responsible   connected   aware

By the end of this lesson you will:

➡ have examined the positive and negative influences in your life

➡ be aware of the way you influence others

KEYWORDS

Influence

Positive influence

Negative influence

 INDIVIDUAL ACTIVITY

Reading for enjoyment and with understanding

Read the following account from a teenage girl, Molly, and then fill in the table by ticking the people and things that influence the decisions she makes about her life.

Molly

'I get the ideas for my clothes from *Grazia* magazine. I changed my hairstyle last year and I based it on my favourite singer. I started wearing make-up this year because my friends all started wearing it too. Make-up is against the school rules but I mostly get away with it. Last week I got detention, though, because I refused to take off my mascara and eye liner. I have toned it down a little now, though, so nobody notices that I am wearing it.

'At the weekend I usually hang around the local shopping centre with my friends and we usually go to McDonald's for something to eat. I just get fries and a soft drink because I am vegetarian since I saw a documentary on TV about animal cruelty. We are all going to the cinema next week to see the new horror film that everyone on Facebook likes.

'My favourite music is indie-alternative – my brother introduced me to it when he was in Third Year. I wanted to take music as a subject at school, but it didn't fit in with my options so my parents pay for me to do it outside school. I am learning to play the guitar and the flute.

'Sophie, my best friend, wants me to join the new drama group after school but I don't really want to because it is run by Ms Ryan, my English teacher, who I don't get on with. Sophie is annoyed with me now, especially since we both want to study drama when we leave school. I really don't know what to do. Jean, my other friend, says I'm right not to go because Ms Ryan is a real pain.

'I used to do athletics last year and I came second in the schools' competition. The coach has asked me to start training again because he says we will have a very good relay team if I go along. I said it to my mam and she says it would be a great idea and a good way to keep fit too. Training is on Mondays and Wednesdays after school so it fits in perfectly.

'It is my birthday next week and I'm getting the latest Samsung Galaxy. I've saved up the money I got for babysitting and my parents are going to give me the rest. I can't wait because Sophie and all the girls have smartphones already. There's a disco on the night of my birthday too and my parents have said I can go. Some of the lads said they will have some beer and vodka beforehand, but I won't touch it. My mam has me warned against it so I'm not chancing it; plus the Gardaí are often about on school disco nights so I'm not going to risk getting caught. I'm really looking forward to the disco.'

What influences Molly?

	PARENTS	FRIENDS	BROTHERS/ SISTERS	TEACHERS	CELEBRITIES	MEDIA	THE LAW
Hair	☐	☐	☐	☐	☐	☐	☐
Clothes	☐	☐	☐	☐	☐	☐	☐
Make-up	☐	☐	☐	☐	☐	☐	☐
Diet and exercise	☐	☐	☐	☐	☐	☐	☐
Hobbies and interests	☐	☐	☐	☐	☐	☐	☐
Leisure time	☐	☐	☐	☐	☐	☐	☐
Drinking alcohol	☐	☐	☐	☐	☐	☐	☐

PAIR ACTIVITY

Learning with others

In pairs, discuss and answer these questions.

1. Who or what has the most influence on Molly?

_____

_____

2. Pick one positive influence on Molly and explain why it is a positive influence.

_____

_____

3. Pick one negative influence on Molly and explain why it is a negative influence.

_____

_____

4. Pick one way in which Molly could have an influence on other people. Give a reason for your choice.

_____

_____

5. Do you think that the influences on Molly are typical of the influences on teenagers in general? Explain your answer.

_____

_____

What are positive and negative influences?

A **positive influence** is something that helps you to do the right thing or to achieve your potential.

A **negative influence** is something that prevents you from doing your best.

It is important to identify the things that influence the decisions you make because this will help you to understand the choices you make.

As you get older, you become more aware of the people and things that influence you. These include your parents, friends, school, the media and the law. It is important to realise that you also influence other people, including your family, your friends, your classmates and your teammates.

Learning with others

PAIR ACTIVITY

In pairs, take turns at trying to influence the other person.
- The influencer should choose something that they believe the other person should do.
- The other person must try to resist the pressure to be influenced.

Examples could be persuading someone to:
- Take up exercise
- Give up smoking
- Take up smoking/drinking
- Buy a product
- Mitch class
- Agree with your opinion on an environmental issue

LEARNING KEEPSAKE

Three things I have learned in this lesson are:

1. _____

2. _____

3. _____

Something that helped me learn in this lesson was:

_____

_____

_____

As a result of this lesson, I will:

_____

_____

_____

_____ has shared this Learning Keepsake with me _____

Name of student   *Parent's/Guardian's signature*

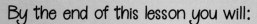

LESSON 31 — Body Image

Learning outcomes: 3.10, 4.2

responsible   resilient   connected   aware

By the end of this lesson you will:

↪ appreciate the importance of a positive body image

↪ identify the influence of the media on our body image

KEYWORDS

Body image

Media

Perception

USEFUL WEBSITES

www.bodywhys.ie Provides support for people with all types of eating disorders.

What is 'body image'?

Body image is a person's perception of how they see their own body, physically and mentally. In simple terms, it is what you see when you look at yourself in the mirror and how you feel about what you see.

A healthy body image is when you accept and appreciate what you look like and all the great things your body can do for you. You are not trying to change your body to fit the ideal you see in the media, online or in your community.

Your body image and your self-esteem (how much you value yourself) are closely linked and can influence each other – your feelings, thoughts and behaviours. If you are not happy with your body (or part of your body), it can be hard to feel good about yourself. The opposite is also true: if you don't value yourself, it can be difficult to feel good about your body and all the great things it can do for you.

WHAT MATTERS MOST IS HOW YOU SEE *yourself*

GROUP ACTIVITY

Learning with others

In groups, brainstorm the pressures, fears and concerns that teenagers face about the way they look. Think about general appearance, weight, build, height, hair and teeth.

BODY IMAGE PRESSURE/ FEARS/ CONCERNS

Body image and mental health

For young people in particular, body image is strongly linked to self-esteem and mental health. Your body is still growing and changing and there can be a lot of pressure from society to conform to a certain image – whether that's to be strong and muscly or thin and pretty. It is important to accept your body the way it is, and to feel comfortable in your own skin, even though it may not match your own or other people's ideals.

Sometimes a quote or a song can get us thinking about our body image. Can you think of any?

> How much time have I wasted on what I look like? Take your time and your talent and figure out what you have to contribute to this world. And get over what the hell your butt looks like in those jeans.
>
> *America Ferrera, actress*

187

I realised that my sole ambition to have the surgery was to appease strangers, to limit their discomfort with my disability and to nudge the dial closer to subscribing to normality. As a child, I wanted to make it easier for people to like me ... I spoke with my parents and my siblings and we came to the conclusion that if people did not like me because I was disabled, because I was a little person, that was their problem, not mine.

Sinead Burke, contributing editor at Vogue

[Brands and marketers] are trying to sell you some unrealistic standard of what a body is when, in actuality, your body is great the way it is. As long as you love yourself and have confidence, I think you won't be fooled ...

Kelvin Davis, male body positivity Instagram influencer

If you retain nothing else, always remember the most important rule of beauty, which is: who cares?

Tina Fey, actress/comedian/writer

I'm not the average girl from your video
And I ain't built like a supermodel
But I learned to love myself unconditionally
Because I am a queen.

India.Arie, singer

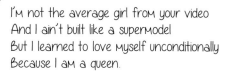

GROUP ACTIVITY

Contributing to making the world a better place; Respecting difference

Imagine you are an editor of a glossy teenage fashion magazine. You have been given the task of changing your magazine to promote positive body image messages. As a group, read the following nine statements and rank them in order of importance by writing them into the diamond graphic on the next page, with 1 being the most important to implement and 9 the least important to implement. If your group have any other ideas, add them to the list.

STATEMENTS
Stop the airbrushing or digital enhancement of images.
Include images of people with a wider range of body types.
Place a greater focus on healthy eating rather than diet features.
Limit the number of images of extremely thin models.
Remove advertisements for cosmetic surgery.
Limit the number of images of muscular men with six packs.
Stop stories that ridicule celebrities because of their appearance.
Include features on a large range of subjects, including jobs and careers, not just on 'how to look perfect' and beauty tips.
Remove articles from bloggers telling young men how to sculpt the perfect body.

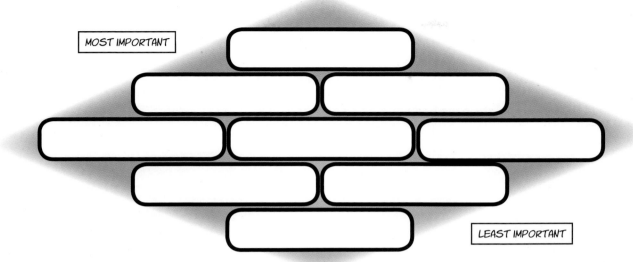

CLASS DISCUSSION

Discussing/Debating

How the media affects our body image

The world is made up of a variety of diverse people of different shapes, sizes and ethnicity. Many of the images that we see in the media do not portray this diversity. This narrow representation of the body adds to the pressure that young people feel when it comes to body image.

Without realising it, we are constantly bombarded with advertisements and images of specific body types on television, social media, food packaging, billboards, magazines ... everywhere we look. If there is something to be sold, we will see a specific body type selling it. People often feel pressurised to fit in with what is considered 'perfect' by the media.

INDIVIDUAL ACTIVITY

Thinking creatively and critically

Examine these images. Can you identify what is being sold in each? Why do you think the people used in the campaigns have been chosen to appear in them?

The media present certain stereotypes of beauty that are not realistic or even attainable. Yet most people find it difficult not to compare themselves to these ideal images. It is important to remember that almost all images used in advertisements, and even images used in films and television programmes, have been airbrushed or digitally enhanced. We do this ourselves when we try to create the perfect selfie. This distorts our true image.

> *To get an illuminating insight into how this is done, go to YouTube and look up 'Dove Evolution' (1:14).*

Body image and social media

- Images we see of our friends on social media impact our body image.

- There is a link between social media and feelings of dissatisfaction with our bodies.

- The images people post on social media are not always realistic. People edit photos to try and replicate what they believe to be attractive.

- Comparing ourselves to others can effect our body image and self-esteem.

- Posting lots of selfies on social media encourages us to focus more on appearance rather than other qualities that make us who we are.

- Social media ensures we have a value attached to our image. The number of 'likes' we get on our pictures can influence how good or bad we feel about ourselves. It may even cause us to remove the picture.

10 STEPS TO A POSITIVE BODY IMAGE

1. Appreciate all that your body can do for you. Your body is amazing.

2. Keep a top ten list of things you like about yourself – things that aren't related to how much you weigh or what you look like.

3. Look at yourself as a whole person; choose not to focus on specific body parts. You are much more than your looks, so pay attention to other areas of your life.

4. Spend time with positive people who accept and appreciate their bodies.

5. Shut down those voices in your head that tell you your body is not right. Build yourself up with positive self-talk.

6. Wear clothes that are comfortable and make you feel good about your body.

7. Become a critical viewer of social and media messages. Try not to compare yourself to unrealistic images in the media.

8. Do something nice for yourself, something that lets your body know that you appreciate it.

9. Don't pay too much attention to how many likes you get on your social media images. It is not an indication of your value as a person.

10. Remember that your body is unique. Your individual differences give you style and personality.

Being confident

INDIVIDUAL ACTIVITY

Reflect on your relationship with your body and how you think about it and treat it by filling in the spaces in the graphic.

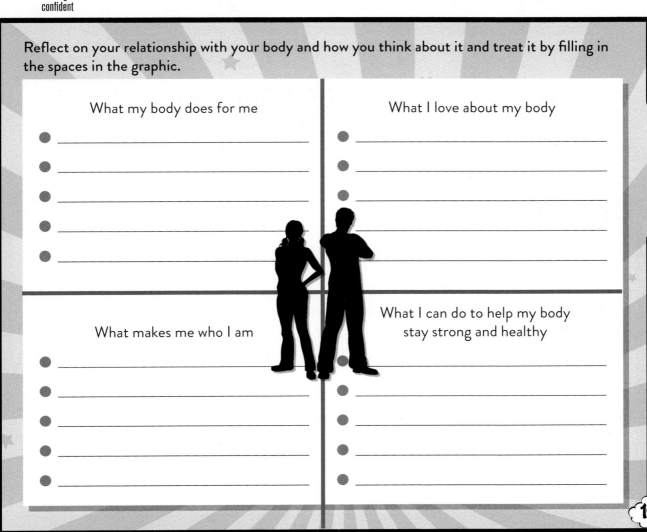

What my body does for me

- _____
- _____
- _____
- _____
- _____

What I love about my body

- _____
- _____
- _____
- _____
- _____

What makes me who I am

- _____
- _____
- _____
- _____
- _____

What I can do to help my body stay strong and healthy

- _____
- _____
- _____
- _____
- _____

191

LEARNING KEEPSAKE

Three things I have learned in this lesson are:

1. _____
2. _____
3. _____

Something that helped me learn in this lesson was:

_____
_____
_____

As a result of this lesson, I will:

_____
_____
_____

_____ has shared this Learning Keepsake with me _____

Name of student   *Parent's/Guardian's signature*

MEET THE CHALLENGE

Strand 4 Topic 1
POSITIVE MENTAL HEALTH BADGES/WRISTBANDS

Learning outcomes: 1.7, 4.1, 4.6

As a class, design a set of five badges or wristbands that promote positive mental health.

○ Discuss and come up with a theme/slogan for your badges/wristbands.

○ Identify helplines/websites that are relevant to mental health and include them as text on the badges/wristbands.

○ Break into five groups, with each group responsible for designing and creating one of the badges/wristbands.

○ Research how to make the badges/wristbands and how many you will need for your year group/school.

○ Distribute the badges/wristbands around your school.

TOPIC 2
Mental Health and Mental Ill-Health

LESSON 32
Understanding Mental Health

Learning outcomes: 4.4, 4.5, 4.6

 responsible
 resilient
 connected
 respected
 aware

By the end of this lesson you will:

•➤ be able to identify mental health issues experienced by young people and/or their family members

•➤ appreciate what it means to live with mental ill-health

•➤ know how to access mental health services in your local area

KEYWORDS

Mental health

Stigma

USEFUL WEBSITES

www.yourmentalhealth.ie Provides information, support and advice on mental health.

www.youthhealth.ie Provides a directory of mental health services available in local areas.

www.samaritans.ie Provides emotional support for people experiencing despair or distress.

www.grow.ie A mental health organisation which works to help people who have experienced or are experiencing mental health problems.

www.jigsaw.ie A free community-based mental health service for 12–25-year-olds. It offers one-to-one support for young people dealing with difficulties.

www.pieta.ie Provides free treatment programmes for people who have suicidal thoughts or who self-harm.

www.mindourminds.ie Search 'help is at hand' for a wide range of mental health services available to young people.

Listening and expressing myself

As a group, discuss what words come into your heads when you hear the terms 'Physical health', 'Physical ill-health', 'Mental health' and 'Mental ill-health' and write them into the table below.

PHYSICAL HEALTH	PHYSICAL ILL-HEALTH	MENTAL HEALTH	MENTAL ILL-HEALTH

Mental health

Just as we all have physical health, we all have mental health. Having a healthy mind and body are both very important. When our body is unwell, we usually know what to do to feel better: we try some remedies, we go to the doctor, or we stay at home and get some rest. Sometimes, however, when our minds are unwell, we may neglect the problem and carry on, not giving ourselves the care we deserve and need. This can lead to problems getting worse.

Mental health is an essential part of our overall wellbeing. It is about:

- being comfortable in our own skin

- having good ways to deal with our feelings

- being confident

- knowing where we fit in

- having a sense of purpose

- being able to manage difficulties and let-downs when they arise

Mental ill-health

Just like physical ill-health, people can experience mental ill-health at different times in their lives. Mental ill-health can range from general everyday stresses, worries or low periods, which are normally temporary, to more serious long-term conditions. Having mental ill-health affects the way we feel, think and act, and it can make it more difficult to do what we want to do in our daily lives. Getting the correct help and support is essential in the journey to feeling better.

GROUP ACTIVITY

Learning with others

In groups, brainstorm different situations that could affect a young person's mental health, e.g. bullying, family problems, etc.

ISSUES THAT MIGHT AFFECT A YOUNG PERSON'S MENTAL HEALTH

Mental health and stigma

Thankfully, nowadays the topic of mental health is more openly discussed. Many young people feel more comfortable talking about mental health issues and know to seek help when they need it. However, some people are still reluctant to seek help when they are feeling overwhelmed as they fear social stigma. Teenagers sometimes feel too embarrassed to admit that they are not coping; they worry that family and friends will judge them or see them as weak or crazy. It is important that we learn the facts about mental health issues so that we can reduce this stigma.

Stigma occurs when people are feared, avoided or looked down on because they are seen, in some way, as different.

INDIVIDUAL ACTIVITY

Knowing myself

How much do you know about mental health? Read these statements and tick whether you think the statement is a myth or a fact or if you are unsure. Your teacher will share the correct answers with you.

STATEMENT	MYTH	FACT	UNSURE
Mental health problems are extremely rare.			
Only adults experience mental health problems.			
Young people with mental health problems are different from other young people.			
Only certain types of people experience mental health problems.			
People with mental health problems are just weak; they can snap out of it if they try hard enough.			
Once a person develops a mental health problem, they will never recover.			
I can't do anything for someone with a mental health problem.			
Mental health problems will clear themselves up on their own in time.			
People with mental health problems are violent and unpredictable.			
Therapy and self-help are a waste of time for anyone with mental health issues.			

CLASS DISCUSSION

Discussing/Debating

Mental health problems that affect young people

ANXIETY

Anxiety is a feeling of fear or panic. Everyone will experience symptoms of anxiety at different points in their lives, but it passes. Anxiety becomes a problem if it is experienced on an ongoing basis and it interferes with a person's life.

ANGER ISSUES

This is when a person's anger is expressed in a destructive or unhealthy way. The anger causes the person to lose their self-control and they can harm themselves or people around them.

EATING DISORDERS

These are characterised by a variety of disordered eating behaviours such as self-starvation (fasting and/or food restriction), purging (self-induced vomiting, over-exercising or laxative abuse) and bingeing (eating more than the body needs to satisfy hunger).

LOW MOOD

This is when a person feels sad or down. The feelings don't normally last long and usually go away after resolving a difficult situation. If the feelings do not go away, a person needs to seek help as they may be experiencing depression.

PANIC ATTACKS

These are sudden feelings of intense fear; they don't last long but they can be very scary.

OBSESSIVE COMPULSIVE DISORDER (OCD)

This is a type of anxiety disorder. It can be serious but it is very treatable. A person with OCD can experience repeating thoughts, images or feelings that make them feel distressed. They carry out habits (compulsions) to help them feel safe from their worries or fears. These habits are called rituals.

Looking after your mental health

There is a wide range of treatments for people with mental health problems, such as talk therapies, medication, support groups and holistic strategies. It is important not to wait until challenges become overwhelming to look after our mental health. The following are examples of different day-to-day things we can do that can make a big difference in maintaining positive mental health.

Keep active: Regular exercise helps improve our self-esteem and self-confidence. When we exercise, 'happy' chemicals known as endorphins are released, leading to a more positive mood.

Share your problem: Sharing how you are feeling with a friend or family member can make a big difference. It can help you get another perspective on things. A problem shared is a problem halved.

Do things with others: Getting involved in group activities – such as joining a team, joining a choir, volunteering – can have a positive effect on how you feel.

Care for someone else: Being helpful and kind to others is a great way to build your self-esteem. A simple act of kindness can make a difference to someone else's day and make you feel better.

Stay in touch: Spending time with friends and family is extremely important for your mental health. It is important to have a strong support system during difficult times.

Be positive: Remind yourself of the positive things about yourself. Don't be too hard on yourself. Embracing and accepting who you are helps to boost your self-esteem. Practise keeping a gratitude diary and each night write down three things for which you are grateful.

Sleep well: Getting 8–9 hours' sleep a night can help you feel better equipped to deal with the next day's challenges.

Take a break: It is important to take breaks and have time for yourself. If you feel a situation is too stressful, take a break from it. Sometimes stepping away from something can give you time to relax and de-stress. This can be going for a run, reading, listening to music, or something else you enjoy doing.

Practise mindfulness or meditate: This involves paying attention to what you are doing in the moment. It can be difficult at the start but you will improve with practice. Whether it is brushing your teeth or eating, you can put all your attention into that activity. Being present in the moment helps us to better enjoy our lives.

When to ask for help

If you are struggling with your mental health, it is important to seek help. If you tackle a problem early, it will prevent it from getting worse. People can and do recover from mental health problems. Taking the first step to getting support can be difficult, but it will be the best move you will make.

- Talk to a friend, family member or someone you trust.

- Talk to a school counsellor.

- Find out about local agencies and the supports they offer.

- Ask your parent or guardian to bring you to a doctor.

LEARNING KEEPSAKE

Three things I have learned in this lesson are:

1. _____
2. _____
3. _____

Something that helped me learn in this lesson was:

_____

_____

_____

As a result of this lesson, I will:

_____

_____

_____

_____ has shared this Learning Keepsake with me _____

Name of student   *Parent's/Guardian's signature*

MEET THE CHALLENGE

Strand 4 Topic 2
SLIDESHOW PRESENTATION ABOUT LOCAL MENTAL HEALTH SERVICES

Learning outcomes: 1.7, 4.4, 4.6

Research local services that offer support and advice to young people on mental health. Select one agency that interests you and prepare a short slideshow presentation about the type of support this agency offers young people. In your slides, include:

○ the name and contact details of the organisation

○ the reasons someone would contact this organisation

○ the type of support offered by the organisation

○ any other information that you think is relevant

LESSON 33

Building Resilience

Learning outcomes: 4.8, 4.9

 responsible
 connected
 resilient
 respected
 aware

By the end of this lesson you will:

•→ understand what it means to be resilient
•→ develop different strategies for building resilience
•→ be aware of the different coping strategies for managing tough times

KEYWORD

Resilience

 **USEFUL WEBSITES**

www.mentalhealthireland.ie Provides information on how to build resilience and improve your overall wellbeing.

www.barnardos.ie Provides a teen help section which gives information about issues affecting young people.

www.childline.ie A 24-hour helpline and online support service offering advice and support to children and young people under 18. **Freephone 1800 666 666**.

What is resilience?

Resilience is the ability to bounce back from setbacks or failures in our lives and regain a sense of wellbeing. Everyone experiences challenges in their lives. Some challenges can be more difficult than others. Just as physically healthy people are better able to bounce back from illness or injury, resilient people are better able to bounce back from difficult situations.

GROUP ACTIVITY

Learning with others

As a group, discuss some difficult situations that young people may experience and write them in on the graphic on the right.

Building resilience

There are many things we can do to build resilience so that we are better prepared to deal with challenges when they arise.

Get 8–9 hours' sleep every night.

Aim for sixty minutes' exercise per day.

Eat a healthy, well-balanced diet.

Use assertiveness skills. Stand up for yourself, learn to say no.

Use humour. Laughter can make us feel good.

Building Resilience

Relax. Take time out. Do things you enjoy; practise mindfulness.

Connect with others. Make time for friends. Join a club.

Try to think positively. See the positive in situations; try not to focus on the negative.

Set clear, achievable goals.

INDIVIDUAL ACTIVITY

Being healthy;
Being confident

Building resilience is like filling a backpack before a journey. You fill the backpack with coping skills in advance so that you are prepared during difficult times. In the backpack, write the things you are already doing in your life to build resilience, e.g. 'I listen to music when I want to relax'; 'I take my dog for a walk when I want to clear my head'. Then, using a different coloured pen, write down what other things you could do to build up your resilience.

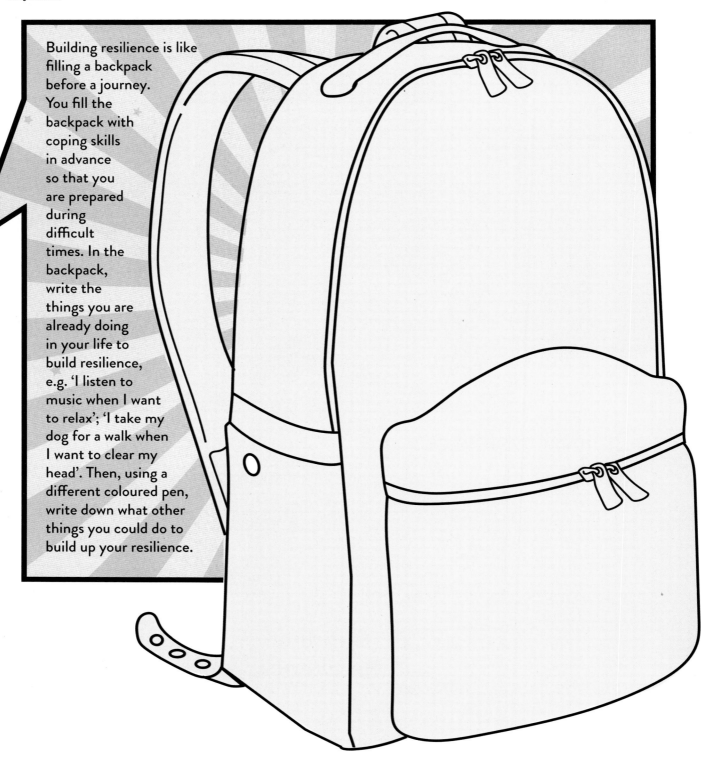

Dealing with difficult times

A basketball is a good representation of resilience. When the ball is full of air, it bounces back into our hands when dropped. Likewise, when everything in our lives is going well and we are happy, we have the ability to 'bounce back' when we hit a low point. If the basketball loses air, however, it will not bounce back so easily when it hits the ground. Similarly, there are some things in life that 'let the air out'. These can be challenges such as bereavement, divorce, moving schools, poor relationships, arguments at home, etc. It is important that we use coping strategies at these times to refill our basketball and get it bouncing again.

The following acronym can be useful to refer to when we experience setbacks in our lives.

Bad times don't last. Things usually get better. Stay optimistic.

Other people can help if you talk to them.

Unhelpful thinking makes you more upset.

Nobody is perfect, not you and not others.

Concentrate on the positives, no matter how small, and use laughter.

Everybody experiences sadness, hurt, failure, rejection and setbacks sometimes, not just you. They are a normal part of life. Try not to personalise them.

Blame fairly. How much of what happened was due to you, how much to others or to bad luck or circumstances?

Accept what can't be changed (but try to change what you can first).

Catastrophising exaggerates your fears. Don't believe the worst possible scenario.

Keep things in perspective. It's only one part of your life.

Dealing with difficult situations

When things go wrong and we are feeling down, there are many things we can do to help us cope. Different things work for different people. There are also unhelpful things we can do that make it more difficult to deal with difficult situations, for example shutting ourselves away in our rooms, eating too much junk food, or playing video games for hours on end.

INDIVIDUAL ACTIVITY

Being healthy;
Being confident

Look at the coping strategies below. Put a line through strategies you think are unhelpful and should avoid, and circle those that you think are helpful.

Start a fight

Say how you're feeling on your social media page

Write about how you're feeling in a diary/journal

Walk the dog

Blame someone else

Sit down and try to come up with a plan to tackle the problem

Do absorbing activities (e.g. crosswords, puzzles) that take your mind off your worries

Use humour

Ignore the problem and hope it goes away

Think of the worst-case scenario

Use negative self-talk

Pretend nothing is wrong

Talk to someone about how you're feeling

Don't eat enough

Contact a help agency

Talk to friends or family members about your problems or worries

Close yourself off and avoid people

Overeat

Meditate

Abuse substances such as alcohol or cigarettes

Take time out and come back to the problem later

Think positive thoughts

Get angry and lose your temper

Worry excessively

Keep busy – try to keep your mind off your worries

Play a game or take exercise

Blame yourself

Foresee the best outcome

IT IS VERY IMPORTANT TO SEEK HELP OR TO TALK TO SOMEONE YOU TRUST IF YOU ARE FEELING DOWN OR WORRIED.
REMEMBER: A PROBLEM SHARED IS A PROBLEM HALVED.

PAIR ACTIVITY

Listening and
expressing myself

1. In pairs, discuss and then write down why you think some people might be reluctant to tell others if they are feeling down or sad.

_____

_____

_____

_____

2. What are the benefits of talking to someone about our problems?

_____

_____

_____

_____

REMEMBER: IF A FRIEND OR A FAMILY MEMBER TELLS YOU THEY ARE FEELING DEPRESSED, ARE SELF-HARMING OR ARE FEELING SUICIDAL, YOU MUST TELL SOMEONE WHO CAN HELP. DO NOT KEEP THIS INFORMATION TO YOURSELF.

INDIVIDUAL ACTIVITY

Knowing myself

To build resilience in difficult times, we need a few key coping strategies that we can use when a challenge comes our way. In the hand, write down five strategies that work for you.

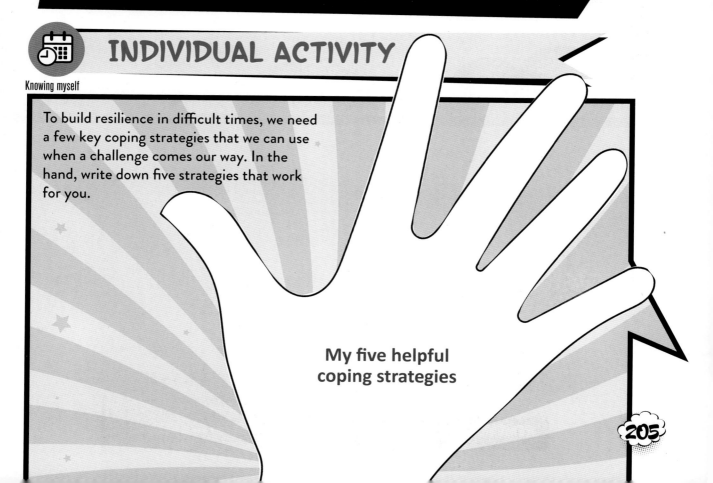

My five helpful
coping strategies

LEARNING KEEPSAKE

Three things I have learned in this lesson are:

1. _____
2. _____
3. _____

Something that helped me learn in this lesson was:

_____

_____

_____

As a result of this lesson, I will:

_____

_____

_____

_____ has shared this Learning Keepsake with me _____

Name of student   *Parent's/Guardian's signature*

MEET THE CHALLENGE

Strand 4 Topic 3

BUILDING RESILIENCE' ARTICLE FOR SCHOOL MAGAZINE

Learning outcomes: 1.1, 4.8, 4.9

Write an article for your school magazine on what young people can do to help build resilience. In your article, include the following:

- ○ what resilience is
- ○ what young people can do to build resilience
- ○ what can help young people to bounce back after a challenging situation
- ○ inspirational quotes
- ○ any other information you feel is important

TOPIC 4
Loss and Bereavement

LESSON 34
The Stages of Grief

responsible   connected   resilient   respected   aware

Learning outcomes: 4.11, 4.12, 4.13

By the end of this lesson you will:

- → recognise that change and loss are normal parts of life
- → understand the five stages of grief
- → learn about the personal, social, emotional and physical responses to loss and bereavement
- → know how to look after yourself and others in times of loss and bereavement

KEYWORDS

Bereavement

Grief

Loss

Change

Ritual

USEFUL WEBSITES

www.childline.ie A 24-hour helpline and online support service offering advice and support to children and young people under 18. **Freephone 1800 666 666.**

www.rainbowsireland.ie A peer support group for people of all ages who have experienced the death, separation or divorce of someone in their lives.

www.teenlineireland.ie A non-profit helpline aimed at young people aged 13–19 years. **Freephone 1800 833 634 or free text TEEN to 50015.**

www.childhoodbereavement.ie Provides guidance and support for young people to enable them to manage the impact of death in their lives. **Tel 01 679 3188 or message them on their website.**

Change and loss

In First Year, you learned that change is a necessary part of life and comes in many forms. Some changes are positive, while others are challenging. For example, for some people, moving from primary to secondary school can be challenging; while you look forward to the challenges and opportunities in your new school, you may also miss your friends from your old class and the school community that you were part of. Similarly, for some people, the loss of a pet might prove very upsetting, while another person will be more accepting of the loss and move on.

Everyone reacts differently to loss; the reaction depends on the individual person and the circumstances.

INDIVIDUAL ACTIVITY

Reading for enjoyment
and with understanding

Read the following poem about how we all sometimes try to avoid 'the elephant in the room' and then participate in a class discussion about it.

'Elephant in the Room'

by Terry Kettering

There's an elephant in the room.

It is large and squatting, so it is hard to get around it.

Yet we squeeze by with, 'How are you?' and 'I'm fine,' and a thousand other forms of trivial chatter. We talk about the weather. We talk about work.

We talk about everything else, except the elephant in the room.

There's an elephant in the room.

We all know it's there. We are thinking about the elephant as we talk together.

It is constantly on our minds. For, you see, it is a very large elephant.

It has hurt us all.

But we don't talk about the elephant in the room.

Oh, please say their name.

Oh, please say their name again.

Oh, please, let's talk about the elephant in the room.

For if we talk about their death, perhaps we can talk about their life.

Can I say their name to you and not have you look away?

For if I cannot, then you are leaving me ...

Alone ...

in a room ...

with an elephant.

Understanding bereavement, loss and grief

Grief is the variety of feelings that a person experiences as a result of loss and/or change. When we lose someone or something that is important to us, we grieve.

Grief can be difficult and unpredictable. The feelings and thoughts of grief come and go in waves as you try to come to terms with your loss while getting on with your day-to-day life. At times, you might feel you are coping quite well, only to experience a burst of grief when you least expect it or are reminded of your loss.

There are five stages usually associated with grief:

1. **DENIAL.** Denial is the body's way of helping us deal with loss. You are in shock and find it hard to believe what has happened. This reaction helps us to survive the loss. Denial helps us to pace our feelings of grief and it is nature's way of letting in only as much as we can handle.

2. **ANGER.** Anger is a necessary stage of the healing process. You feel angry about what has happened and that it has happened to you. You may take your anger out on those closest to you.

3. **BARGAINING.** At this stage you may enter into bargaining in an attempt to return your life to the way it was before. You may say things like, 'I promise, if they get better/if everything works out OK, I will never again ...'

4. **DEPRESSION.** As reality begins to set in, you can have feelings of emptiness and despair. You may feel grief at a deeper level. Acknowledge that this is an appropriate response to a great loss.

5. **ACCEPTANCE.** You accept what has happened and acknowledge that you can and will find a way to learn to live with your loss.

Grief is a process of healing, and so it is important to know that each stage is an important step to recovery. However, it is also important to know that these stages aren't necessarily worked through in this order, nor is every stage necessarily experienced. You might repeat some of these stages, or not experience them at all. Grief is a different experience for everyone. Feelings of regret or guilt or relief might also happen. No feeling is wrong. What is important is that you talk about your feelings if you are feeling overwhelmed, and know that everyone experiences grief in their own way.

Remember:

Grief is a process; it takes time.

Everyone's grief is different.

There is no right way to grieve.

Strong emotions and thoughts are part of grief.

Responses to loss and bereavement

Loss and bereavement affect your physical and emotional wellbeing and can also have an impact on how you interact socially, emotionally, physically and spiritually.

- Social responses relate to how you interact with others and they include withdrawal from social events, isolation, risky behaviour, obsession with the deceased, avoidance of reminders of the deceased and increased use of alcohol and drugs.

- Emotional responses include poor concentration, absent-mindedness, confusion, forgetfulness and surreal feelings.

- Physical responses affect our body and how it functions and they include nausea and chest pains.

- Loss may pose challenges to your spiritual beliefs, e.g. faith in God.

Learning with others

The word wizard below contains common responses to grief and loss. Identify which responses are physical and which are emotional by writing them into the clouds on the next page.

PHYSICAL EFFECTS

EMOTIONAL EFFECTS

How to care for yourself and others

Caring for yourself

Grieving is a very individual process and what others find helpful may not work for you. This is a list of suggestions that may be helpful.

- Be gentle with yourself and kind to yourself. You determine the pace of your grieving process. Everyone's response to grief is different, so avoid listening to other people telling you how you should feel and when you should feel it.
- Allow yourself to feel the grief.
- Expect that your concentration at school will be affected.
- Talk to friends or family about your grief.
- Self-care is important. Healthy eating, exercise and sleep are essential.
- Consider keeping a journal to write down how you are feeling.
- Read books or poetry, both to distract you and to comfort you.
- Plan and engage in social activities. It is OK to go out and have a good time.
- If someone offers you help, accept it. Tell them what it is you would like/need.
- Carry a memento of your loved one if you find it helpful.
- Join a school group such as Rainbows, where you can talk to other people and share your loss.
- Take a yoga class as a way of practising relaxation and self-care.
- Give of yourself by helping someone else.
- Write down what life is teaching you. Try to learn from life's lessons, however difficult they are.

Caring for others

Helping others can aid your own healing process. The following are some suggestions for helping someone who is grieving.

- Be a good listener; be available and accepting.

- Avoid telling them how they should be feeling during their grief.

- Remember and acknowledge special anniversaries, celebrations and activities and be particularly supportive during these special and important times.

- Exercise patience.

- Be aware that it is necessary for them to go through certain stages of the grieving process.

- Encourage self-care such as healthy eating, regular exercise and sleep.

- Treat them to nice things or do something nice for them.

- Include them in events and trips.

- Let them talk about the person who has died.

- Don't be frightened of bringing up the name of the person who has died, or try to avoid mentioning them or anything to do with them because you are afraid of upsetting the bereaved person by reminding them of their loss. The chances are they are thinking about this person and would welcome the opportunity to talk about them if they feel like it. Don't ignore 'the elephant in the room'.

- Don't worry about 'saying the right thing' – there is no right thing to say in this situation. The important thing is to be there for someone who is grieving, to support them however you can, and to let them talk about or feel their feelings of grief as they need to.

 # INDIVIDUAL ACTIVITY

Reading with understanding

Read the following story about Ezra and then participate in the class discussion afterwards about it.

Ezra

Ezra is fourteen and lives at home with his mother and two sisters. He is popular at school, involved in many sports and an important member of his local rugby team. He also participates well in class and is very much up for a laugh. Sadly, Ezra recently lost his dad after a long illness. At first, he seemed to cope with his loss, and his classmates and teachers were very supportive and looked out for him. However, in the last few weeks he has become introverted, angry, short-tempered and often silent. He has started to miss rugby training, is distracted in class and is beginning to avoid his friends and is not interested in going out when they call.

CLASS DISCUSSION

Discussing/Debating

LEARNING KEEPSAKE

Three things I have learned in this lesson are:

1. _____
2. _____
3. _____

Something that helped me learn in this lesson was:

_____
_____
_____

As a result of this lesson, I will:

_____
_____
_____

_____ has shared this Learning Keepsake with me _____

Name of student   *Parent's/Guardian's signature*